Gompas in Traditional Tibetan Society

Gompas in Traditional Tibetan Society

by

M.N. Rajesh

Decent Books
New Delhi

Published and printed by:
Decent Books
D-36/A-1, Mohan Garden
Najafgarh Road
New Delhi - 110 059

Distributed by:
D.K. Printworld (P) Ltd.
Regd. office : *'Sri Kunj'*, F-52, Bali Nagar
New Delhi - 110 015
Phones : (011) 545-3975, 546-6019; *Fax* : (011) 546-5926
E-mail: dkprintworld@vsnl.net

ISBN 81-86921-21-4

First Published in India in 2002

Acknowledgements

I WOULD firstly like to acknowledge the Central Asian Studies Division, School of International Studies, Jawaharlal Nehru University and my guru Prof. Dawa T. Norbu for encouraging me to work on the *gompas* of Tibet.

I take this as an opportunity to thank my friends Bakil Alwallss, Ravi Ranjan Prasad and Sanjeev Kumar for their help in going through my manuscript and suggesting necessary changes. Harpal Singh and P. Sekar also helped me as good friends in making this research see the light of the day by their constant inspiration and also Noorul Hoda.

Thanks are to P.N. Suresh Kumar of the Government Museum Chennai, and Dr. K.P. Rao, Reader, Dept. of History, University of Hyderabad for helping me with the map. I would also like to thank the staff of the JNU library, Lobsang and Debbie Smith of the Tibet House Library, New Delhi. Pema Yeshe and the staff of the Library of Tibetan works and Archives, Dharamsala helped me to access relevant material. I would also take this as an occasion to thank M. Ganesha and the staff of Connemara Public Library, Chennai for taking pains to source old books and lend them. Zhang Zhongqun and Ram Ashray of the Library of the Chinese Embassy, New Delhi, also helped me by lending books not available anywhere.

Above all I would like to thank my family members for bearing with my long absence from home.

Contents

Introduction

THE *gompa*s were one of the central institutions in pre-modern Tibet which is an extensive area of study in terms of time and space. The time period extends from roughly the seventh century AD to AD 1959 and the geographical area too is equally immense comprising all of Tibet, Mongolia, Bhutan, parts of India, China, Nepal and Central Asia. Buddhism is an institutionalised religion and the *gompa* was the institution which led to the continuance of Buddhism throughout the major part of Tibetan history. Earlier trends in the study of *gompa*s focussed mainly on the architectural and artistic aspects without taking into account the social context and the institutional aspect of the *gompa*.

This study tries to look at the *gompa* from a holistic view focussing mainly on the organisational and functional aspects. The major areas of enquiry are the Indian antecedents of the *saṁgha*, its evolution into the famed multi-functional *mahāvihāra*s of northern and eastern India which formed the prototype for the Tibetan *gompa*. The subsequent proliferation of *gompa*s in Tibet in the favourable ecozones, with a brief description of the material base of the *gompa* and its relation with the superstructure, i.e., the society. The material base would also help in classifying the *gompa*s from a typological point of view. The second diffusion of Buddhism in Tibet saw the proliferation of *gompa*s and the emergence of large-scale monasticism. This is a grey area with very little research being done and some aspects of the spread of monasticism during this period are being looked into.

Functionally the services rendered by the *gompa* to the people, viz., education, medicine, astrology and astronomy form another area of enquiry. Here the emphasis is on the socio-economic linkages with the community. Earlier works had emphasised heavily on the Indian antecedents leading one to conclude that Indic sciences were just translations of Indian works. An attempt at delineating the local contributions which suitably modified these sciences and 'Tibetanised' them to suit the needs and specifities of the times have been touched in this chapter. Further Western travellers had arrived at conclusions that the system of education was of a mystic and esoteric kind, giving a picture that Tibetan monastic sciences served to this end. The practical role of medicine, astrology and astronomy in everyday life has been discussed here.

Further, Gelugpa monasteries and their system of education have been the subject of many works and here an attempt is made to show the different types of education in other Orders.

Closely linked to monastic education was the internal organisation of the monastery. Here also a typological classification has been attempted giving a description of the working of the great monasteries with thousands of lamas and their roles in the rituals, the hierarchy, regulations and rules, right from the recruitment and initiation of the novice, to the office of the abbot, covering the entire gamut of positions of authority.

Monastic art was not for art's sake only and keeping this paradigm in mind the religious and surrogate uses of art have been discussed. Various styles of art and the rise of a national style (like the coalescence of various schools of medicine into a national school) have been traced in a linear fashion. Further the uses of art and the *gompa* as a repository of art and architecture perpetuating a pan-Tibetan great tradition performing the vital role of integration have been detailed.

Large-scale monasticism with the socio-economic linkages forms another chapter and merits a discussion. So the role of *gompa* in the socio-economic process has been examined describing briefly the assets of the *gompa/labrang,* their incomes, surplus and reinvestment of surplus in various fields.

The concept of merit and the social context that prompted the laity to donate to *gompa* are also touched upon. The redistributive role of the *gompa is* also shown.

Monastic input into polity is a major theme on which Tibetologists are working on now. Here the early polity of Tibet, the Śākya polity and the rise of Gelugpas are traced. The contentious Yon-chod relationship and the factors leading to the rise of the theory of reincarnation are also dealt with. A brief description of the system of the Dalai Lama's government is also given. Contributions of the monastery in infusing and later implementing a polity based on the Buddhist concept of *ahiṁsā* leading to the elimination of use of force as a matter of policy is also touched upon.

A brief survey of literature

The primary sources for this study are the *Vinaya* Texts and the *Blue Annals.* For tracing the Indian antecedents particularly in reference to the origin of the *saṁgha,* Indic sciences and monastic education, the *Vinaya* Texts are helpful. The *Blue Annals* are particularly used in tracing the developments in Tibet to supplement the secondary works. It has been pointed out by many scholars that only the *Blue Annals* and Bu-Ston Rinpoche's, *History of Tibet* stand out as relatively fair portrayals of historical events as they do not tend to gloss over or use hyperboles in abundance, which was a trend among the Asian works of that age. Moreover, the dates and events mentioned in the *Blue Annals* correspond to conclusions arrived out of later independent research.

Among the secondary works, some books like R.S. Sharma's *Material Culture and Social Formations in Ancient India* give a clear picture of the material milieu of early Buddhism following the model of the base and superstructure. Sukumar Dutt's book *Buddhist Monks and Monasteries of India* is a fairly exhaustive work describing the organisational features of the great Indian *mahāvihāra*s and also throwing light on Indo-Tibetan contacts. O.C. Handa's *Buddhist Monasteries of Himachal Pradesh* also is in the same vein tracing a teleological link between the Indian monasteries and the monasteries of Himachal Pradesh up to this day, dwelling upon all aspects of monasticism, very similar to this work is Romi Khosla's *Buddhist Monasteries in the Western Himalayas* which introduces us to the geographical terrain of the western Himālayas and the rest of the book is concerned with the architectural aspects of the monasteries. Janet Rizvi's book *Ladakh Cross Roads of High Asia* can be said to supplement this book but with a more diverse range of subjects concerned with Ladakhi society and its historical moorings.

The contributions of travellers, administrators and early Tibetologists like Charles Bell whose *People of Tibet*; *Religion of Tibet* and *Tibet Past and Present* along with Tucci's *Tibet Land of Snows,* Sir Thomas Holdich's *Tibet the Mysterious* acquaint the reader with an introductory knowledge of Tibet and its customs, myth and folklore. *Ancient Tibet* (Tibetan History Series, V) gives exhaustive details about early Tibetan history, topography and natural resources.

Regarding Indic sciences, Raoul Birnbaum's *The Healing Buddha* and Kenneth Zysk's *Asceticism and Healing in Ancient India* give a theoretical overview about the connection with Buddhist monasticism and healing, both authors stress upon the organisational role of the early *saṁgha.* Lady Dr. Lobsang Dolma Khangkar's *Lectures on Tibetan Medicine*; *Fundamentals of Tibetan Medicine* published by Men Tsee Khang help to get a knowledge of the basis of Tibetan medicine. Dr. Lobsang Rabgay's articles and Dr. Pasang Yonten's articles along with a few others in *Tibetan medicine* help in tracing the history of Tibetan medicine along with the myths and their modifications. Dr. Jan Barmark's article, 'Tibetan Buddhist medicine from the perspective of Anthropology of knowledge', gives a clear picture of the orientation of the Tibetan mind and the role of after life, it also touches briefly on the training of a doctor. Craig R. Janes's article and Sirish Jain's article give information about the medical practices in Lhasa (Chakpori) and among the Bodhs of Spiti.

Articles by Dr. Sonam Wangdi and Dr. Philip along with the collection of articles in *Tibetan Astronomy and Astrology — A Brief Introduction* more than suffice the need for a description an Indic sciences.

'The Geshe Degree', Daniel Perdue's *Debate in Tibetan Buddhist Education,* Michael Franz's *Rule by Incarnation,* Austine Waddell's *Buddhism of Tibet or Lamaism.* T.L. Shen and S.C. Liu's *The Tibetans* give a good overview of monastic education and organisation, stressing on the organisational hierarchy, process of recruitment, maintenance of discipline, etc. 'The structure of the Gelug Monastic Order' an article by Sherpa Tulku *et al.* also does justice to its title. Kunchok Sithar's article takes us down on a journey through time to compare monastic life in the past and present.

Regarding art and architecture there are a plethora of books and articles, some like Romi Khosla's and O.C Handa's work being region specific, i.e., Western Himālayas. Pema Dorji's, book *Stupa and its Technology* goes into a brief discussion on the origin and symbolism of the *stūpa,* as Robert. E Fisher's *Buddhist Art and Architecture.* William Semple's article on 'Symbolism and Ritual in Tibetan Architecture' along with Thubten Legshay Gyatsho's *Gateway to the Temple* explain in detail the techniques and ritual procedures of construction, the latter book also gives the meaning of myths and iconographic canons. Pratapaditya Pal's *Tibetan Paintings* goes into detail about the stylistic changes in Thanka painting articles edited by Pratapaditya Pal in *Marg* also do justice by dealing with each aspect of Tibetan art ranging from Jane Casey Singer's description of Thankas, and Valrae Reynold's article on fabric images that stresses the role of fabric images in Tibetan society. Detlef Ingo Lauf's *Tibetan Sacred Art* deals with the concept of *maṇḍala,* and tāntric motifs elaborately. Ven Melpittiye's, doctoral thesis is useful in analysing the shifts in symbolism from Theravāda to Mahāyāna Buddhism. Krishna Ghosh's doctoral thesis titled *'Few Tibetan Dieties'* goes in great detail to trace the origin of certain selected deities always emphasising their historical and functional context.

On the socio-economic front, the overview given by Charles Bell *et al.* can be expanded by David Snellgrove's *A Cultural History of Tibet,* R.A. Stein's *Tibetan Civilisation* which stress on the cultural aspects and bears the imprint of the 1960s when cultural studies came to the fore. Robert James Miller's *Monasteries and Culture Change in Inner Mongolia* also belongs to this genre following a descriptive and narrative theme. Namkhai Norbu's book *The Necklace of Gzi: A Cultural History of Tibet,* though not bulky gives an interesting reinterpretation of Tibetan myths and culture stressing the 'Bonpo' roots of Tibetan culture Paljor Tsarong's doctoral thesis on the *labrang* examines the economics of a monastic estate in Ladakh using the Marxist analysis of modes of production. Ugen Gombo's article on traditional Tibetan economy introduces us to the various facets of production and consumption in old Tibet. Leonard R. Chapela's article and Thomas Wiley's articles on economics take the same subject to much deeper lengths. Melvyn Goldstein's article 'On Reexamining Choice Dependency and Command in the Tibetan Social System' discusses about the role of *miser* and serf in the Tibetan production system.

On polity, Franz Michael gives a description of the Tibetan political system from a Weberian Point of view. Ram Rahul's works, *Dalai Lama The Institution,* and *Government and Politics of Tibet* go into full detail about the working of the government of the Dalai Lama. Geoffrey Samuel's *Civilized Shamans* examines Tibetan Buddhism and polity using the categories of clerical and Shamanic practices as bipolar opposites. Tsepon W.D. Shakahpa's book *Tibet: A Political History* chronicles the history of Tibet from earliest times making good use of original sources with a lengthy discussion on the Yon-chod relationship. Reginald Ray's article, 'Some aspects of the Tulku tradition in Tibet', takes off from this point to trace the development of the institution of Tulku and rise of the institution of Dalai Lama and the functions of the Tulku. Dawa Norbu's *Tibet The Road Ahead* has an annexure, 'Transformation of a Warrior Nation' which explains the shifts in political ideology and the role of Buddhism in shaping Tibetan polity.

1

Geographical Locations and the Origins of the Saṁgha

TIBET, 'the roof of the world', 'the land of snows', 'the land of the lamas', 'the lost Shangri-La', has been described as a mystic land nestling in the vast outback's of the Himālayas. Being highly inaccessible, accounts of travellers and missionaries have only accentuated the mystique around this land. Partly because the average traveller never fully explored the diversities of Tibet, and the unique facets of Tibetan society. This only led to the portrayal of Tibet as a place where time stood still.

The people of Tibet call their country as Bod, though some scholars link it with Bon, the earliest religion of Tibet, evidence being inconclusive. Indians have always referred to Tibet as Bhot or Bhot-desh, Ganjong or Kwachen, meaning 'the abode of snow' and Sildanjong meaning the cool climate land, are the other names by which Tibet is known. The modern name Tibet derives from the Mongolian Thubet, Chinese Tofan and more specifically from the Arabic Tubbat.[1]

The Tibetan physical cultural and ethnic boundaries are all not the same and over the centuries have been constantly redrawn and therefore have to be seen against the background of its history.[2] Today Tibet has an area of 1.2 million sq km, which works out to roughly one-eighth of the total

---

1. Tsepon W.D. Shakabpa, *Tibet — A Political History,* 1967, p. 1.
2. Tsung Lien Shen and Shen Chien Liu, *The Tibetans,* 1953, p. 9.

land area of the Peoples Republic of China.[3] This area is called the Tibetan Autonomous Region. However, the Qamdo prefecture in neighbouring area is also almost Tibetan. But the scope of this study lies beyond the present-day boundaries which focuses on pre-modern Tibet, encompassing Ladakh which was a part of the western Tibetan Guge Kingdom and parts of Nepal, Mongolia, Sikkim, Bhutan and parts of India.

The logic of including the above-mentioned areas in this study is that they are all Tibetan culture areas. Though the spoken language of the above-mentioned regions may be mutually unintelligible, the monastic customs and the linkages of the *gompa*s here to the mother monasteries in pre-modern Tibet and the uniformity of monastic rules, customs, beliefs and literature with minor variations, lead us to include them in the 'Tibetan Culture area'.

The core area of our study is the Tibetan plateau, bounded on the north by Xinjiang, the territory of the Uighurs, Qinghai on the north-east, Sichuan on the east and on the south, Hunan. To the south and west are Myanmar (Burma), India, Bhutan, Nepal and Sikkim.[4] In Nepal the Dolpo and Mustang regions are the Tibetan culture areas whereas Bhutan is entirely Buddhist with the exception of Nepali Hindu settlers who also predominate in some parts. Sikkim, now an Indian state is also dominated by Nepali Hindus, the rest being the Bhotias and Lepchas who profess Tibetan Buddhism. In northern India, Ladakh and Zanskar valleys in the Indian state of Jammu and Kashmir, and Lahaul, Spiti and Kinnaur in the adjoining state of Himachal Pradesh, both having borders with the Tibet Autonomous Region are Tibetan culture areas. In the north-eastern frontier of India is the Indian state of Arunachal Pradesh also bordering the Tibet Autonomous Region, of the Peoples Republic of China, here we find enclaves of Tibetan culture areas.

The major physical features dominating the Tibetan

3. *Tibet — The Roof of the World — China Facts and Figures,* 1990, p. 1.

4. *Ibid.*

landscape are the ChangTang, Tsaidam basin, southern Tibet, north-eastern Tibet and south-eastern Tibet. The Tibetan plateau is the result of the upheaval of the earth's crust resulting in the elevation which is at an altitude of 17600 ft at the 79th meridian going to about 13000 ft in the north, and relatively comfortable 11000 ft in the Southern Zone[5] are the northern plains extending from 80° E to 92°E longitude and from 31°N to 36° North latitude.[6] This is one of the toughest areas in the whole of the world where human survival is a great test of endurance. The notable features of this vast plain which covers a considerable part of northern Tibet are low rainfall, which is less than 4 cm a year, high velocity winds, often exceeding 45 miles per hour creating dust storms and erosion. The harsh climate is at its severest in the winter when temperature drops down to – 35°C and is accompanied by severe frost. The temperature can also vary from as high as 30°C in the day to as low as – 5°C at night in summers, thus resulting in hot spells in the day and abrupt cold at night.

Snow doesn't fall to the ground but gets evaporated on account of the dryness. The rivers here are glacier fed and melt in the summer while in the winter they are completely frozen. The topography of ChangTang can be said to consist of weathered gravel and pebbles due to the erosive action of wind and frost with some shrubs at favourable places like the edges of the lakes and mountain slopes with supply of water. The picture improves as one moves south-ward where there is more grass due to relatively greater rainfall.[7]

Another feature which strikes us is the large number of salt water lakes, that are the source of salt which, till recently, was an important item of trade, borax and soda, that are often found in a crystalline form.[8] The high amount of solar radiation and absolute conditions of cold, coupled with

5. Thomas Holdich, *Tibet the Mysterious,* 1904, p. 34.
6. *Tibet — The Roof of the World,* n. 3, p. 3.
7. *Ancient Tibet* (Tibet History Series V, 1986), pp. 55-6.
8. Tsung Lien Shen, n. 2, p. 16.

dryness, make it nearly impossible for anything to grow on this landscape except grass[9] which is found in abundance in the southern regions of ChangTang, where one also finds some game like the wild yak, wild ass (Tib: *kiang*), wolves, antelopes, leopards, sheep and even gazelles. The low resource base makes it fit only for the nomads to live in this vast pastureland. To the north of ChangTang are the highest peaks of Kun Lun and this is the area which demarcates the Tibetan cultural sphere, as one finds mixed populations of Mongols, Hor people (Hor pa) further north.[10] On the whole, it can be said that the ChangTang is a low density populated region with extremes of temperature and physical features ranging from desert like conditions in the north to more favourable conditions in the south, with pastoralism being the main form of production. The true desert is found in Tibet in the Tsaidam basin (46000 sq miles) which lies in the north-eastern corner and is a barren, almost waterless region, save for the occasional lakes around which some white willow and vegetation is found. Tsaidam is rich in coal, oil, borax, soda, potash, gold and silver. It also supports some scrubby vegetation.[11]

Next is north-eastern Tibet which is characterised by a rugged landscape set amidst a mountainous terrain. This is the Amdo region and also the area of the fierce Goloks, a pastoral area inhabited by nomads famed as fighters.[12] Next is southern Tibet that is also called Central Tibet as it has the Central Ü province on the valley of the Tsang-po and its tributaries. It is sometimes called Ü Tsang to imply the closeness between the two administrative divisions Ü and Tsang which were the political and cultural centres of Tibet and also wherein Lhasa the capital is located.[13]

---

9. *Ancient Tibet,* n. 7, pp. 50-64.
10. R.A. Stein, *Tibetan Civilisation,* J.E. Stapleton Driver, tr., 1972, p. 23.
11. *Ancient Tibet,* n. 7, pp. 56-7.
12. Charles Bell, *The People of Tibet,* rpt. 1991, p. 4.
13. *Ibid.*, p. 3.

The Gangdise and gNyan-chen-thang-lha in the north and the Himālayas in the south bound the region. This is a more hospitable region in terms of climate with more warmth and moisture but temperature fluctuates from as low as —7°C in winter to 16-30°C in summer, when this region receives rainfall of around 20-40 inches. In the western part of this region around Gor-thag, the scene is somewhat different with cold dry climate and low rainfall. As one moves east, the climate becomes moist and warm and vegetation also increases from the alpine type of steppes on the Gangdise ranges to true forests with poplar, fir and other coniferous trees in the river valleys east of Lhasa. As one descends even more south, tropical forests are encountered, full of animals like geese, finches, magpies, leopards, monkeys, wild cats and many more other animals.[14] One of the main reasons for the conducive conditions is the fall in elevation which tapers down from a high of around 15000 ft at the point where the Tsang-po (Brahmaputra), (Indus) and (Sutlej) divide to the east and west to about 13000 ft near Ladakh in the west and 11000 ft near Lhasa the area of the *Bodyul* or settled inhabitants.[15]

The most populous area of Tibet is the south-eastern Tibet where the Khams province is located. It is the most forested of all the provinces ranging from moss, grass and shrub to pine and oak in the colder regions, mixed forests of birch, oak, hemlock, etc., in the warmer, wetter regions down south.[16] The striking feature of this region is that due to the ruggedness of the terrain, each valley has a slightly different climatic condition. The fertility of this area is because of its elevation that at times reaches down to 6000 ft making such places unfit for human habitation due to the narrowness caused by erosion. Most settlements are at around an altitude of 9000 to 13000 ft above sea level. Along with agriculture and forest produce, we also find deposits of gold, silver, copper, lead

---

14. *Ancient Tibet,* n. 7, pp. 57-8.
15. Thomas Holdich, n. 5, p. 18.
16. *Ancient Tibet,* n. 7, pp. 59-60.

and iron.[17] One also does not face any severe extremities of weather, here and the climate, as a whole is salubrious in nature.[18]

Before we move to Ladakh, a word about Tibetan agriculture. The ChangTang plateau is used only as a pastureland, with good quality of grass high in nutrients. Alpine grasslands are also found in Khams and Amdo. Goats, yak, sheep and horses are the main animals thriving here with sheep in the west and a good number of horses in Amdo and Khams.

Agriculture is possible in Tibet on the plateau, which is at a great height absorbing large amounts of solar radiation, which in turn heats up the air close to the ground by radiation from the land. Barley is the main staple crop along with wheat followed by millet. Cold resistant highland barley can be grown even at an altitude of 15500 ft. Rice, maize and vegetables are found only at lower elevations in the central valleys and farther down south at lower elevations. The Yarlung and Tsang-po rivers, Nyog-Chu, the rDza-Chu and the Bri-Chu have the best agricultural lands.[19] The Yarlung valley is the centre of the settled agricultural areas.

The area called western Himālayas or sometimes referred to as Lamaist Himālayas to mark out the Buddhist culture areas, consists of Ladakh, Zanskar Lahaul and Spiti, all of which were at times part of the polities of western Tibet, significantly during the second diffusion of Buddhism.

Ladakh was not part of the Dalai Lama's territories, though most of the Gelugpa *gompas* here were subject to Potala, but was ruled by a Gyalpo who claimed ancestry from a Tibetan royal family, and he was assisted by some local rulers. While eastern Ladakh and Zanskar are Tibetan Buddhist, western Ladakh and Baltistan (now administered

---

17. Tsung Lien Shen, n. 2, p. 16.
18. Thomas, Holdich, n. 5, p. 19.
19. *Ancient Tibet,* n. 7, pp. 61-2.

by Pakistan) have been Islamicized.[20]

Lahaul, Spiti and Kinnaur, though a part of the western Himālayas are in the Indian state of Himachal Pradesh; here one can see the continuity of Mahāyāna Buddhism unbroken for almost a thousand years (e.g., Tabo monastery which recently celebrated its centenary in 1996 AD) due to their isolated location.[21]

In western Nepal, the Tibetan people are present in Dolpo, the small Tibetan kingdoms of Mustang and Jesib. Among the Tibetanised people are the Thakkali people of Tak who are a partly Tibetanised and partly Hinduised people professing trade and are mainly found in the upper Kali Gandahi Valley. Other Tibetan peoples are the people of Tsum, Nob-ri, Nar-p'u and Gyasmundo. In eastern Nepal the Sherpas of Rolwaling, Khumbu and Solu are some of the most researched groups by anthropologists.[22]

The Himālayan kingdom of Bhutan, the land of Thunder Dragons is a small land locked country with an area of 47000 sq km, two-thirds of it being forested and much of the country being mountainous. Bhutan also has diversities in weather ranging from intense cold in the north to sub-tropical to tropical conditions in the south. The Thimpu and the Paro valleys are the most productive areas and also the most populous.

Bhutan had associations with Tibet from as early as the time of Songtsen Gampo and Padmasambhava. Drugpa sect is the most popular sect, unlike the Gelugpa sect that is popular elsewhere. Though there are three main languages which are mutually incomprehensible, the national language is Dzongkha, derived from the Ngalong people whose cultural affinities are more closely related to Tibet, the Dzongkha

---

20. Geoffrey Samuel, *Civilized Shamans Buddhism in Tibetan Societies,* 1993, pp. 111-13.
21. O.C. Handa, *Buddhist Monasteries in Himachal Pradesh,* 1997, pp. 5-9.
22. Geoffrey Samuel, n. 20, pp. 108-10.

language is closest to the standard literary Tibetan. In its pre-modern period Bhutan was a part of the Tibetan culture area, a fact evident by the two temples out of 12 built by Songtsen Gampo to exorcise the indigenous spirits that one located in Bhutan.

Sikkim, presently an Indian province, too, like Bhutan is non-Gelugpa with the majority being Nyingmapas. Like Bhutan, Sikkim also had hoary associations with Tibet from the time of Padmasambhava. There are two main ethnic groups here: the Tibetan (or Bhotia) and the 'indigenous' Tibeto-Burman-speaking people, partly Tibetanised called the Lepchas. The ruler of Sikkim till 1974 was the Chogyal whose predecessors generally maintained good terms with Lhasa.[23]

Other Tibetanised areas in India include parts of Arunachal Pradesh where the Monpa of the Tawang Corridor live. Here we also find the famous Tawang monastery, a large Gelugpa *gompa* and, it was also the birth place of the sixth Dalai Lama in 1683. Along with the Monpa, the Lopo and Sherdukpens are also found. A host of minority ethnic groups previously ruled by petty kings and partly Tibetanised populations are also found in small numbers on the other side of the Indian border in the Tibet Autonomous Region of the Peoples Republic of China.[24]

The vast Tibetan Culture Area with many diversities, are conditioned by altitude, rainfall, source of water and landscape, all peculiar to each locale; often we find enclaves that are strikingly different from the general pattern in an area, i.e., like an oasis in the desert. Some other examples would be of the fertile valley of Dro-Mo in Tibet with forested hillocks and a vale of flowers set amidst craggy hill ranges[25] or the Nubra valley with poplars in Ladakh.[26]

In Tibet proper there was a four-fold division of land

---

23. Dillip Bhattacharya, *Bhutan,* 1975, p. 17.
24. Geoffrey Samuel, n. 20, pp. 103-4.
25. Thomas Holdich n. 5, p. 18.
26. Janet Rizvi, *Ladakh Crossroads of High Asia,* 1996, pp. 32-3.

based on its usage. They were reffered to as (1) the Tang, which are the uncultivable plains and valleys at very high elevations, (2) Gang are the ridges as well as the cultivated plains; and these ridges are mostly in Eastern Tibet; (3) The Drok are the grazing grounds; and (4) The Rong are the valley areas that are mostly found in the south where Tibet touches the Himālayas. It is also important to note that these different classes of land are more often combined in the same region.[27]

This functional division of land is found in many other pre-modern societies,[28] leading to diverse ways of life, reflected in occupational patterns, variations in dialect, literary genres, cultural motifs and in short the whole societal process itself. In pre-modern Tibet, characterised by low density of population and relatively isolated settlements there developed many local traditions. The unifying aspect was the *gompa*, which symbolised the Tibetan Great Tradition. To illustrate this the Tibetans had coined a proverb 'every lama has his own method of teaching and every valley its own mode of speech'.[29] This was what led to the two primary forms of subsistence in pre-modern Tibetan society. The agriculturists (*shingpa*) and the pastoralists (*drogpa*), though one also found some *Samadrog* who combined agriculture by maintaining some herds of animals.[30]

Based on these parameters and with primary focus on the distribution of the *gompa*s, the settlements were categorised by Geoffrey Samuel as centralised agricultural communities, remote agricultural communities, pastoral communities, and urban communities and may hold valid.[31]

---

27. Sir Charles Bell, n. 12, p. 2.
28. The Tinai concept of five-fold division of land was followed in Tamil Society during the Sangam period.
29. Pratapaditya Pal, *The Art of Tibet,* 1969, p. 13.
30. Geoffrey Samuel, n. 20, p. 41.
31. *Ibid.*, pp. 115-16.

Origin of the Buddhist saṁgha

The context in which the Buddhist *saṁgha* had originated conditioned its aims and structure to a considerable extent. Prince Siddhārtha Gautama later the Buddha was born in Kapilavastu amongst the Śākya clan of which his father Śuddhodana was the ruler. As prophesied earlier the Prince saw a decrepit old man, a diseased man, a dead body and finally an ascetic. These four sights prompted the Prince to think beyond the portals of royal luxury within which he had till then spent his entire life. He renounced the world and became a wanderer in search of the ultimate truth.

This was the period in Indian history which is referred to as the second urbanisation to signify the evolution and growth of cities in eastern and near north-eastern parts of India, corresponding to modern-day eastern U.P. and Bihar (i.e., the Gangetic valley area). A marked feature was the growth of state system with a stratified social class and failure of the kinship based tribal Vedic system to adjust to the new situation. Increased production led to affluence in agriculture and crafts saw the emergence of a new elite based on this material progress. The rice economy and iron deposits fuelled this process as rice could support a much larger population and a good number of the people could now devote entirely to crafts without bothering about food production. This new elite were the *gahapati*s who were household cultivators often owning immense tracts of land and merchants who are mentioned in the *Jātaka*s as having a caravan (*sārtavāha*) of a thousand carts.[32] Vedic Brāhmaṇism failed to co-opt this elite, who along with the kṣyatriyas, who were the ruling classes, were also the patrons of the new sects. The kṣatriyas detested the brāhmaṇas as they acted as a check on royal absolutism and appropriated power. Another factor was the sudden change in the economy which left many people stupefied as they lost their moorings in a changing society, they had not envisaged. In this context there were around

32. R.S. Sharma, *Material Culture and Social Formations in Ancient India,* 1992, rpt., pp. 120-31.

63 sects ranging from the orthodox Vedic to the materialist Cāravākas, Agnostic, Upaniṣadic, Ājivakas, Nirgranthas, etc. — all seeking solutions to the myriad problems of human existence.

This trend of non-conformism was prevalent from the day of the later Vedic period by the *vrātya*s and gained many adherents by the Upaniṣadic age and there are ample references in the *Bṛhadāraṇyaka Upaniṣad* and the *Muṇḍakopaniṣad* about *bhikṣu*s or wandering almsmen. The young prince Siddhārtha also set-off on this line practising 12 years of gruelling austerities, which included acts of self-mortification that made him an emaciated figure standing on death's door. Like many other recluses, the young prince Siddhārtha had embarked on one of the paths that was widely prevalent and finally came to the conclusion that it was useless. He now concentrated on meditation and after ardous meditation for four weeks in which he overcame the temptations symbolised by the demon Māra, he finally attained enlightenment or Buddhahood under the *bodhi* (*pīpal*) tree at Bodh-Gayā and tenceforth came to be known as the Buddha, or the enlightened one.[33]

One of the main tenets, the Buddha expounded was the middle path which preached the avoidance of extremes, i.e., gross materialism on the one hand and rigid austerities on the other hand. This was a departure from the Upaniṣadic *bhikṣu* whose abstract doctrine and practices clearly had no link with the laity and during the time of the Buddha, the *bhikṣu* was a part of the society, yet detached from materialist bondages. He was now an intelligible human figure whose philosophy struck a common chord among the humanity.

Buddhism at the bottom is an ethical and a compassionate religion and the Buddha preached that it was incumbent on every follower to have compassion for all sentient beings. Going by this line of thought the goal of the individual was not salvation only for him which was to be

---

33. C.V. Joshi, 'Life and Teaching' in P.V. Bapat, ed., *2500 years of Buddhism*, 1997, p. 21.

attained in an ethical way, but also the liberation of the millions and thus to liberate these millions the monastic system originated. The Buddha himself had implored the monks:

> O' monks, go on a round for alms to different places. Dont go twain to the same place to preach the *dharma*.[34]

To proclaim the pure and holy life the monks themselves had to set a moral example and in this regard the primary function of the monks was to preserve the Doctrine and thus preserve Buddhism as such, then to spread the Doctrine amongst the masses. The monastic community became a coherent entity to respond to the challenge of the brāhmaṇas, with whom they engaged in lot of disputations.

Suffice to say here that the popularity of Buddhism and consequent patronage after the *mahāparinirvāṇa* of the Buddha led to increased prosperity. By this time (6th century BC) the rules had been codified in the first Buddhist Council held at Rājagṛha. The *Vassavasa*[35] which was a rain retreat and adopted from the *parivarjaka*s was given canonical injunction by the Buddha and it was during the rainy season that the monks had to stay at one place. This signalled the start of a sedentary life, and with the rise of strong states with equally strong kings like Aśoka of Magadha, support was forthcoming and the monks were generally provided with food, clothing and shelter. Patronage to the Buddhist *saṁgha* (monastery) came both from the royal persons and from the laity.

Folk elements and aspects of worship made the *stūpa* an object of intense devotion and congregation and signalled the incorporation of the *stūpa* and *caitya* as an integral part of the monastery. By the 1st century AD, the concept of *bodhisattva* a feature of Mahāyāna Buddhism also led to popular ethos and the Great Tradition interacting, resulting

34. C.V. Joshi, 'Life and Teaching' in P.V. Bapat, ed., *2500 years of Buddhism,* 1997, p. 30.

35. *Ibid.*, p. 25.

in a new form which has been designated variously as 'Vajrayāna', Tāntric Buddhism.

During the period *c.* fourth century AD, onwards great monasteries or *mahāvihāras,* aptly called monastic universities, evolved, which concentrated mostly on academic pursuits attracting talent from far and wide both from within and outside the country especially Sri Lanka, China, Thailand, Burma (Myanmar), Srivijaya, Tibet,[36] etc. The most renowned among them were the monasteries of Nālandā, Vikramaśilā, Valabhī, Jagaddala, Somapura, Oḍantapurī, Ratnagirī, Kānherī, Dhanyakaṭaka, etc., most being located in or near north-eastern India, i.e., the lower Gangetic valley (modern-day Bihar and Bengal) and western and southern India. This was the situational context from where Buddhism was introduced to Tibet and these were the monasteries, which provided the model for the establishment of monasteries in Tibet.

In the Mahāyānist Buddhist context the monastery or *vihāra* is known by the name of *dgon-pa (gompa* plural) in Tibetan. The Tibetan dictionary gives the etymological explanation of *dgon* meaning wilderness, fig tree, a hermitage, a solitary place, so-called on account of its situation in earlier times in lonely isolated places abounding in *bodhi* trees.

Tibetan history generally has two landmark events, one regarding the origin of the Tibetan people who, it is believed according to ancient folklore descended from the union of a monkey and an ogress.[37] The other important milestone is the accession and period of Songtsen Gampo, and the second point is the building of the first monastery at Sam-ye. The historians being mostly Buddhists considered these events as important from a Buddhistic point of view. From Songtsen Gampo's time Tibetan contact with the Indian *mahāvihāras*

36. Sukumar Dutt, *Buddhist Monks And Monasteries of India,* 1962, p. 342.

37. Namkhai Norbu, *The Nechlace of Gzi — A Cultural History of Tibet,* 1989, p. 3.

started leading to cultural interaction between India and Tibet. Later writings have stressed the antiquity of Bon, the prevalent religious tradition of Tibet prior to the introduction of Buddhism, the point of emphasis here being that the Tibetans were not a wild and uncivilised people before the introduction of Buddhism.

But Tibetan history has much more antiquity and to put it in a nutshell, there existed neolithic[38] communities in Tibet as shown by the findings from the sites of Luk, lha-rtse, Yarlung. There was also the kingdom of Zhangzhung which is identified with western Tibet, i.e., the area around Ngari. 'Shamanic' beliefs were prevalent in pre-Buddhistic Tibet and it goes to the credit of Lord Shenrab Miwo of the Shen stock, whom recent scholars identify as having systematised the earlier Shamanistic beliefs in addition to his own Bon teachings.

Tibet was exposed to Buddhist influences from Central Asia, India, Nepal and China. But the institutionalised form of monastic Buddhism started during the reign period of Songtsen Gampo, who was influenced by his Chinese wife Wencheng and Nepalese Queen Bhr̥kuṭi Devī converted to this religion and thus began the spread of Mahāyāna Buddhism in Tibet.[39]

To trace the rise of monasticism it becomes necessary to trace coeval developments in the political sphere and in this respect Songtsen Gampo, Trisong Detsen and Ralpachen stand out, as they are, the three big names associated with the establishment of Buddhism in Tibet.

Early Tibetan history is shrouded in mystery and in the sixth century we come to the reign of Namri Songtsen who according to tradition was the thirty second in the line of rulers who started with Nyatri Tsenpo. Namri Songtsen (*c.* AD 570-619) was one of the early Tibetan kings who ventured beyond the Yarlung valley which was the traditional base to

---

38. *Ancient Tibet,* n. 7, pp. 90-4.

39. Charles Bell, *The Religion of Tibet,* 1992, rpt. pp. 33-5.

as far as the Chinese border subjugating several Qiang tribes to which Sui accounts testify. Large areas of Central Tibet fell to his army which was known to have consisted of a lakh warriors.[40]

This tradition was further continued by his illustrious son Tri Songtsen better known as Songtsen Gampo (*c.* AD 617-50) who became the king in AD 629 at the tender age of 13. He started on an expansionist spree and a diplomatic mission was sent to the Nepalese king Aṁśuvarman, headed by his minister GarTongtsen and the Nepalese king gave his daughter Bhr̥kuṭi Devī in marriage to Songtsen Gampo,[41] which was evidently a marriage of convenience. The second marriage in this series was with WenCheng the Chinese princess who was won after a show of arms to defeat the ruler of TU-Y U-HUN (Eastern Tartars) who was also a claimant to the princess's hand.[42] The Chinese too consented after a battle that went in Songtsen Gampo's favour. Besides subduing the Chiang, Pailan and Tang- Hsian tribes he reached as far as upper Burma (Myanmar) and parts of Nepal besides keeping the Chinese at bay. Songtsen Gampo is known as the first religious king Cho-gyal (Skt. *dharmarāja*) and it is his achievements in the field of religion which are remembered more than his military exploits. His queens Belsa (the Nepalese princess) and Gyalsa (the Chinese princess) brought with them an image of Akṣobhaya Buddha and an image of Śākyamuni respectively, both images said to have been blessed by the Buddha himself, and due to the efforts of his queens Tibet's earliest temples Jokhang and Ramoche were founded. Religious culture was given a further impetus when Songtsen Gampo sent his minister Thonmi Sambotha to India to devise a script for the Tibetan language, which led to Thonmi Sambotha's journey to Kashmir where he learnt Sanskrit and acquainted himself with Brāhmī and Gupta scripts, leading to the birth of the Tibetan script 'lentsa' based

40. *The Blue Annals,* Part One, George N. Roerich, tr., 1949, pp. 47-8.
41. *Ibid.*, pp. 49-50.
42. *Ibid.*, pp. 49-51.

on the Gupta script.[43] Buddhist religious works including *The Secret* were now translated. Even during this time (*c.* 7th century AD) there was Bon-Buddhist rivalry.

Songtsen Gampo's successors were not as illustrious as him and constant warfare plagued Central Asia, with the Uighurs and Tibetans allying at times to defeat the Chinese and gain control of the Silk route. It was left to Trisong Detsen (AD 742-97) who continued to patronise Buddhism, and also had to deal with the anti-Buddhist Bon-party at the Court which led to purges of some influential pro-Bon courtiers and ministers.

Trisong Detsen the second Cho-gyal can be said to have given Buddhism a firm footing. Like his predecessor Songtsen Gampo, Trisong Detsen's long rule was marked by extension of Tibetan arms which reached as far as the Chinese borders and even supported a puppet emperor. He is remembered in Buddhist history for being the first king to start the monastic tradition in Tibet with the founding of Samye, Tibet's first monastery at around *c.* AD 799. In this sacred mission, the first step was to invite Śāntirakṣita and on whose idea came up the monastery of *Migyur lhungi dubpai Tsuklakhang* 'meaning the temple which is an unchangeable, perfect Mass', which is commonly referred to as Samye. Samye was modelled on the lines of the great monastery of Oḍantapurī that was laid out in the design of a Buddhist universe. But it was easier said than done as this herculean task could not be accomplished at one go by Śāntirakṣita who had come on the young king's invitation from Nepal, where he was on a mission to spread the *dharma*. But Śāntirakṣita received such a cold welcome from the Tibetan masses who interpreted his arrival which was coincidentally accompanied by storms, floods and lightning as bad omens that displeased the spirits forcing Śāntirakṣita to beat a hasty retreat.[44] Before retreating he suggested to the king, to invite Padmasambhava, the great Indian Tāntric master to visit Tibet, which the king dutifully

43. *The Blue Annals*, p. 39.

44. *Ibid.*, p. 43.

did. Bon spirits opposed Padmasambhava's missionary efforts in Tibet. He did not vanquish them but co-opted the Bon spirits into the Buddhist pantheon in a new form of syncretism where primacy was given to Buddhism and at the same time the accommodation of local spirits as 'subordinate' deities served to strengthen Buddhism by gaining the unstinted loyalty of the adherents of folk/Bon religion.[45] It speaks of the genius of Padma-sambhava who being well versed in the magical arts of Tāntric Buddhism was fully able to comprehend the objective reality in Tibet. Equipped with powerful formulas and rituals, Padmasambhava was able to subdue the vissicitudes in the process. Samye soon became a centre of learning where the principal preoccupation was the translation of the large corpus of Buddhist literature into Tibetan language.

There was a trial of seven monks trained by Śāntirakṣita[46] to know if the Tibetans could become good monks and the initial batch of seven proved to be so successful that many Tibetans became monks. This can be said to have heralded a new era in Tibetan Buddhist monasticism. From this stage Tibetan monasticism took off and it was better placed than Indian monasticism as it was modelled on the lines of great monasteries with multifarious functions and did not have to evolve through a long process as Indian monasteries had to, encountering many problems during the various stages of evolution.

Another historic event of religious importance to have occurred during the time of Trisong Detsen was the great debate that took place between the Chinese and Indian traditions of Buddhism. The former was represented by Hoshang, a Chinese monk and the latter by Kamalaśīla, the main contention being enlightenment which according to the Chinese could be attained instantaneously, while the Indian

45. *The Blue Annals.* The spirits who troubled Padmasambhava later became part of the Buddhist pantheon are the twelve guardian goddesses (bsTan-ma bcu gnis).

46. *Ibid.*, p. 43.

school was of the view that enlightenment was a slow gradual process a view that finally emerged victorius. On this eve a proclamation was issued by the king to mark the victory of Kamalaśīla. The main feature of this proclamation was that the 'three Jewels' of Buddhism should never he abandoned. Besides, the proclamation promised unstinted support for the establishment and maintenance of temples.

Ralpachen (AD 806-38) was the third religious king who in addition to being a strong ruler like his predecessors quite unlike them maintained cordial relations with China. A pillar in front of the main gate at Jokhang is testimony to the peace treaty concluded between Ralpachen and the Chinese Emperor in AD 821.

Ralpachen's period witnessed the arrival of the three Indian *paṇḍits*, Śīlendrabodhi, Dānaśīla and Jinamitra. Ralpachen built new temples at Onchang Pou 30 miles from Lhasa on the bank of the Kyichu for which many artisans, silversmiths, blacksmiths, bricklayers and carpenters came from China, Turkestan and Nepal. He also instituted the first monastic taxation system in Tibet wherein every monk was to be provided for by seven households.[47] Another of his creations is the still intact, Yarlung temple of Kachu.[48] Ralpachen fell victim to court intrigue by his elder brother Langdarma around whom the proponents of Bon grouped together. What followed according Buddhist annals was a period of persecution and anarchy. Langdarma's name had become so infamous that a number of folk tales have sprung around him depicting him as a hideous black-tongued monster with two plaits on his head to hide his horn.[49] Buddhism was wiped out from Central Tibet leading to a mass exodus of monks to Amdo in the north-east. Thus, the first chapter of Buddhism and the heroic age of religious kings Cho-gyals came to an end.

Monastic tradition was now kept alive by individual

47. O.C. Handa, n. 21, p. 119.

48. *The Blue Annals*, pp. 43-5.

49. Norbu Chopel, *Folk Culture of Tibet*, 1983, p. 16.

groups of monks who were bonded strongly than ever and with a common purpose to revitalise Buddhism. But this task was to be left to Yeshe Ö, one of Langdarma's descen-dants and the ruler of the Guge kingdom in western Tibet.

The kings of Guge championed the cause of Buddhism and western Tibet and by extension western Himālayas which was then a part of Guge saw an efflorescence of Buddhist activity with the building of innumerable temples and *chortens,* the most famous of these *gompa*s were the ones at Tholing the principal monastic institution of Guge, Alchi, Tabo which are the surviving ones.[50] Tradition says that a total of 108 temples were built by Rinchenzangpo, the master translator, protege of Yeshe Ö. The number 108 appears to be a conventional number and Buddhist mythology, like its Hindu counterpart, is replete with instances of such numbers as 108, 1001, 10,0000, etc., and so doubts are expressed over the actual number of monasteries built by Rinchenzangpo. This effloresence of Buddhism is called the Second Diffusion of Buddhism and apart from Rinchenzangpo the prominent personages associated with this revival were Atiśa[51] (AD 982-1054) from the Vikramasila University.

Buddhism was now firmly anchored and it is at Tabo and Alchi that we see the continuity for almost a thousand years (Tabo AD 996-1996). Atiśa's follower Dromtonpa established the Kadampa sect meaning (one of the Doctrine) away from the Nyingmapa sect (one of the old) which was the earliest as they felt its practices had degenerated. New Kadampa monasteries was established, the most famous ones at Reting in Central Tibet (AD 1056) Drolmalhakang at Netang (AD 1045-54), Sangphu Nentak (AD 1073), Langtang (AD 1093) and Yerpa Drobde (AD 1047).

This was the period of rise of Tibetan masters who visited India before the umbilical cord was to be cut by the Muslim invaders in India, eastern India being particularly affected in the twelfth century. Among these famous teachers was

50. *The Blue Annals*, pp. 68-74.

51. *Ibid.*, p. 72.

Marpa. the teacher of the famous poet-philosopher Milarepa. Marpa visited Nālandā monastery to study under Naropa its abbot and brought back many texts. Milarepa's disciples Gampopa in particular founded the Kagyu lineage that was also to split later. Many Kagyu monasteries were founded in the twelfth century and by this time the Śākya sect founded by Kon Chogyal Pho (AD 1034-1102), was well established in central western Tibet.

Splits occurred due to disputes over points of monastic discipline and canonical law. The subsequent centuries saw the monasteries being involved in temporal matters and were fortified to escape raiders. The focus of monasticism once again shifted to the river valleys of central Tibet with Kham province also witnessing some activity. Western Tibet — particularly the provinces of Ngari and Rudok deteriorated and many of the *gompa*s were abandoned due to falling population and desertion by the villagers, and up to this day it is only the ruins which are, by archaeological standards, considerably well preserved due to the arid atmosphere that are the only historical evidences available to us.

There are many favoured locations to build a *gompa*. All monastic manuals elaborately deal with the selection of site for a *gompa* and in this process geomancy and ritual have contributed to the building tradition. An ideal site should contain water, and if it has streams on the left and right sides or forcing a body of waterfall, then they are called natural attributes. Keeping these ritual and practical considerations, the latter arising out of the favourableness of an eco-zone, one notices the spread of *gompa*s in favourable eco-zones while in the unfavourable ecozones they are a rarity or do not have the grandeur.

A survey of the spread of *gompa*s would illustrate the above point better. First, all scholars are not agreed on the exact number of *gompa*s in pre-modern Tibet with estimates varying to as high as 4000. In the official register at Lhasa in 1882, the following details were noted by S.C. Das. The total number of Gelugpa *gompa*s is 1026 with 491,292 monks, and the distribution pattern being 281 *gompa*s in Ü and Tsang, 150 *gompa*s in the districts of Khyan, Labrang and Kongpo, 27 to Upper Kham and 154 to lower Kham and 414 to Pari chen or greater Tibet.[52] The number of *gompa*s of all the sects would he over 2500.

Another list gives the number of Nyingma *gompa*s and *ani-gompa*s in Tibet as follows:

Nyingma *gompa*s in Ü and T Sang 394[53]
Nyingma *ani-gompa*s in Ü and Tsang 206
Nyingma *gompa*s in DoTod 281
Nyingma *ani-gompa*s in DoTod 8
Nyingma *gompa*s in Do Med 324

Yet another list gives the total number of monasteries belonging to all sects in pre-modern Tibet as 3688.[54]

From the above distribution pattern it becomes clear that the *gompa*s have the highest concentration in central-ised agricultural communities and urban centres, the latter which could be counted on fingertips, viz., Lhasa, Gyantse, Shigatse, Derge, Batang, Litang, etc. Remote agricultural areas had small *gompa*s which were also few in number while large *gompa*s were found in the Yarlung Valley of Ü and Tsang and lower Kham, which had a relatively higher density of population and surplus.

Conclusion

A survey of the geographical distribution of the *gompa*s on the accompanying map would best illustrate the above-mentioned assumptions. Almost all the big *gompa*s like Sera, Ganden, Drepung, Śākya, Tashilhunpo, Hemis and Phyang were located in areas of high agricultural productivity characterised by a stratified society consisting of monks,

52. S.C. Das, 'The Monasteries of Tibet', rpt. from *JASB*, 1905, pp. 106 ff. in *Tibetan Studies,* ed. Alaka Chattopadhyaya, 1984, p. 220.

53. Lama Paltu/Jampal Lodoe, *Record of Nyingma Monasteries in Tibet,* n.d., pp. 1-139.

54. *Tibetan Review*, vol. 11, no. 9, September 1976, p. 23.

artisans and traders apart from the agriculturists. Evidently these areas also had direct access to long distance trade routes and medium-sized towns such as Lhasa, Gyantse, Shigatse, Leh, Kangding or Kandze where the merchants converged. Contrasting to this pattern of the relatively prosperous eco-zones were the more marginal agricultural areas with medium-sized *gompa*s such as Derge, Litang parts of Bhutan and Amdo, though enclaves of prosperity here also had large *gompa*s like Punakha Dzong in Bhutan, Kumbum and Labrang in Amdo. The remote agriculture pattern is found in parts of western Tibet, Amdo, Kham, Dolpo and Mustang regions of Nepal with small *gompa*s. At the farther end are the pastoral areas covering ChangTang, large parts of Amdo, western Tibet, Ladakh which did not boast of any *gompa*s but had religious missions as the nomads were not sedentary.

Primarily a religious institution, the *gompa* performed multifarious functions, therefore, it proliferated or say, was consciously patronised in the centralised agricultural and urban areas for a variety of reasons. As an agent of agrarian expansion, as an institution for legitimising the royal ideology during the Cho-gyal period and later the ideology of the different Buddhist sects. It was the Yarlung valley which emerged as bone of contention between the Karmapa and the Gelugpa sects in the period twelfth-fourteenth centuries AD. Areas like Ngari show *gompa*s that fell into disuse due to lack of patronage and depopulation thereby reinforcing the argument of a correlation between rich and potentially rich eco-zones and the location of *gompa*s. As we shall see in a later chapter, major trade functions were performed by *gompa*s on account of some of them being situated on trade routes they emerged wealthier (e.g., Gyantse, Hemis in Ladakh, Labrang monastery in Amdo).

Below is given a map (on page no. 29) detailing the distribution of *gompa*s (Buddhist and Bonpo)

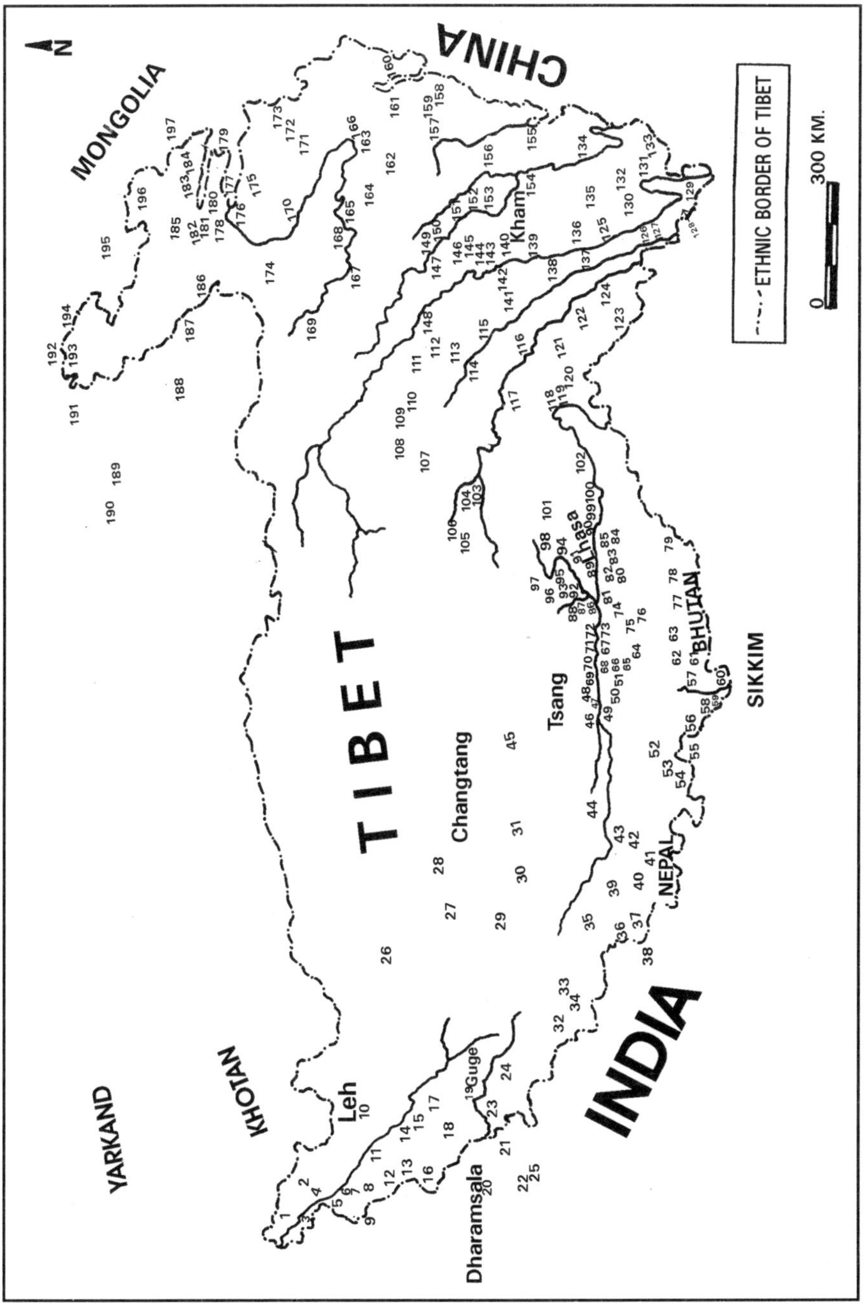
N
MONGOLIA
CHINA
YARKAND
KHOTAN
TIBET
Changtang
Tsang
Kham
Lhasa
Leh
Guge
Dharamsala
INDIA
NEPAL
BHUTAN
SIKKIM
ETHNIC BORDER OF TIBET
0
300 KM.

List of Gompas as given in the Map

The numbers given in the map correspond exactly to the numbers and names given here.

1. Dark Chung
2. Dongkhor
3. Skardu
4. Hanu
5. Kargil
6. Lamayuru
7. Shargol
8. Rangdum
9. Suru
10. Drangtse
11. Hemis
12. Zangla
13. Bardan
14. Phug-g'a
15. Kordzog
16. Repag
17. Wamle
18. Kyi
19. Samur
20. Rewalsar
21. Rampur
22. Dolanji
23. Kanam
24. Tholing
25. Thopgyal-Sarpa
26. Rungmar
27. Kundo
28. Nagrong
29. Selephug
30. Lungkar
31. Mendong (Tso Chen)
32. Shingpheling
33. Khorlhag
34. Tingkar
35. Tchiyor
36. Shugtsal
37. Dorpatan
38. Salyan
39. Lowo Matang
40. Muktinath
41. Nagtsa
42. Mu
43. Dzongka
44. Chatu
45. Zangden
46. Shindarding
47. Jonang
48. Tanag

49. Phunstoling
50. Narthang
51. Ngor
52. Rongphug
53. Namche
54. Jumbesi
55. Jiwang
56. Walung
57. Gangtok
58. Rumtek
59. Darjeeling
60. Kalimpong
61. Paro
62. Phari
63. Punakha
64. Khangmar
65. Gyantse
66. Zhalu
67. Kyilphug
68. Tashilhunpo
69. Shigatse
70. Menri
71. Yungdrung Ling
72. Yungdrung Ling
73. Rinpung
74. Nakartse Dzong
75. Ralung
76. Lhalung
77. Tongsa
78. Lhuntse Dzong
79. Tawang
80. Samding
81. Dorje Drak
82. Mindroling
83. Yarlung
84. Lhagyari
85. Tsethang
86. Tropu
87. Drepung
88. Tsurphu
89. Samye
90. Densatil
91. Ganden
92. Sera
93. Phenpo Nalendra
94. Yerpa
95. see no. 93
96. Taglung
97. Reting
98. Drikung
99. Gyatsa
100. Dvagla Gampo
101. Gyamda
102. Tselha

103. Driru
104. Sok Dzong
105. Shakcuka
106. Tashiling
107. Garsha
108. Tashi
109. 'Adza Sumdo
110. Zahor Dzogchen
111. Surmang
112. Khampagar
113. Karma
114. Riwoche
115. Chamdo
116. Tsawa Pasho
117. Shobamdo
118. Showa
119. Senge Dzong
120. Shing-gi
121. Shugden
122. Sangngak Chodzong
123. Shikathang
124. Menkong
125. Dechenling
126. Yartri
127. Balung
128. Dongakrong
129. Satam
130. Dokardzong
131. Tharlam
132. Mili
133. Yanyuan
134. Barong
135. Do
136. Sampel Ling
137. Tsakhalo
138. Gartok
139. Batang
140. Samar
141. Drayab
142 Konjo
143. Rinagjangsum
144. Palyul
145. Kathog
146. Palpung
147. Dzongchen
148. Drolma Lhakang
149. Tengchen
150. Beri
151. Trewo
152. Drango
153. Nyarong Dzong
154. Nyakcu Dzong
155. Dartsedo
156. Rongdrak

157. Barkham
158. Tsawakhalo
159. Kargu
160. Zungphen
161. Murge
162. Ngawa
163. Metsang
164. Dome Gogma
165. Tarhang Gonpa
166. Sogtsang
167. Doyung
168. Bagchen
169. Khar Rishodbarma
170. Arig Rabgya
171. Lhamo
172. Khar Chagtse
173. Cone
174. Balsa Gonpa
175. Rongpo Gon
176. Trikhakhar
177. Enchung Nam Dzong
178. Ja Kyung
179. Dentig
180. Kumbum
181. Shara Koto
182. Tongkhor
183. Ziling
184. Martsang Lhamo
185. Bar Koto
186. Azha Khar
187. Dulan
188. Kurlyk
189. Balgatai
190. Kar-ri
191. Lungwang
192. Suchou
193. Jayang
194. Chenkor
195. Mathase
196. Bawo Gon
197. Talung Gonpa

2

Gompa and Indic Sciences

MEDICINE, astronomy and astrology are the Indic sciences, which attained a high level of development in Tibet. The above systems of knowledge are referred to as Indic sciences due to the fact that the base of all these three systems had their origin in established Indian systems of knowledge which under went a metamorphosis by incorporating local specificities and external influences, notably Chinese, set against the background of advanced Buddhist philosophy, that gave an overall meaning to the concept of lifeworld to the Tibetan. These three Indic sciences were also in tune with the thinking and philosophical basis of everyday life, ideas and worldview.

The literary elite in Tibet were the monks and naturally it was under their devoted attention that the Indic sciences scaled new heights, with new translations and technological advances. The monks doubled up as doctors and astrologers to amolierate the physical and mental problems of the laymen. The very fact that these systems had survived unbroken till recently was because they were functioning from the *gompa* which was never starved of funds and manpower and, therefore, enriched the tradition continually.

Like other aspects of Tibetan cultures, viz., writing and religion, the same controversies surface when we deal with Indic sciences. The basic question again being that whether the Tibetans were an uncivilised people who lacked the rudiments of culture? This is inexplicably connected with the arrival of Buddhism, and as devout Buddhists, Tibetans have credited most of their achievements from the time Buddhism came to Tibet and ascribing the origins of many aspects of their culture to India. Namkhai Norbu illustrates with clear examples how this trend had come upon in Tibet.[1] It may be said in extension of this argument that even in India many local cultures have histories written from a Sanskritic point of view as many tribal peoples in the course of evolving to state societies sought a 'Great Tradition' from the prevalent Purāṇic Sanskritic mythology. In Tibet also the rise of a 'state society' was co-eval with the establishment of Buddhism (*c.* 7th century AD) and the Tibetan Great Tradition has many Buddhist elements with Indian origins.

The ordinary Tibetan approached illness with a sense of religious convictions and a belief of magic together with the most advanced medical ideas from India, China, and Iran.[2] Thus, medicine was not an autonomous discipline as it is now in Western societies but part of a whole and in understanding the illness, socio-religious practices cannot be divorced, which is how the medical literature came to be imbued with so much religiosity.

The Tibetan system of healing is known as gSo-ba Rig-pa or the science of healing, and it is generally attributed to the Buddha himself in his manifestation as the Buddha of medicine (Skt.Bhaiṣajyaguru, Tib. Sangye Menla).

Buddhist accounts further go on to say that the three previous Buddhas (preceding Śākyamuni) also taught medicine to their disciples. The origin of Tibetan medicine according to Buddhist mythology differs very little from *Āyurveda*, and medicine is first said to have spread in the realm of Gods, then in India or the human realm and finally in Tibet. Here the parallels with Indian mythology are striking. It is said that once the gods desired immortality and along with the demi-gods with whom they were warring

1. Namkhai Norbu, *The Necklace of gzi — A Cultural History of Tibet,* 1989, p. 5.
2. Giuseppe Tucci, *Tibet Land of Snows,* J.E. Stapleton Driver, tr., 1967, rpt., p. 166.

continuously came to know of a vase of nectar deep in the ocean and Rāhula the leader of the demi-gods saw the vase. It was then decided amongst themselves that the gods and demi-gods would together churn the ocean using Mount Meru as a stirring rod and the *nāgas* (serpents), as a rope held on one side by the gods and on the other by the demi-gods who churned together, during the course of which Halā-hala the poisonous snake whose breath contained 409 diseases and was virtually unstoppable appeared. At this instance Brahmā recalled the teachings given by Śākyamuni and uttered the *mantra HUṀ*, on hearing which Hala immediately disappeared. The story later follows the Indian prototype wherein the nectar is restored, and Brahmā passes on the medical knowledge to 'Dakṣa Prajāpati who continues the lineage down to the Aśvins' and from them to Indra who taught them to the sages in the human realm.[3] From this period we get a clearer historical picture, and Bharadvāja the legendary Indian sage is said to have received the knowledge from Indra to cure terrifying diseases which had proliferated among mankind causing misery. Bharadvāja's disciples included Ātreya whose works are embodied in the *Caraka-Saṁhitā* from which one can get an idea to place Baharadvāja in the historical period, i.e., 800 BC. Another famous disciple was the celebrated Dhanvantari around whom many tales have been composed, who along with a host of other disciples totalling eight composed the commentary known as *Caraka-Saṁhitā,* though controversies reign to this day regarding the author-ship of the *Caraka-Saṁhitā*.[4] Other important historical personalities revered in both Indian and Tibetan systems of medicine were Suśruta, the surgeon and author of *Suśruta Śalya Tantra* who lived around sixth century BC and Nāgārjuna who revised Suśruta's works lived around the fourth century BC and is the founder of the Mādhyamika school of philosophy. Some scholars view Nāgārjuna, the author of various medical texts and one of

---

3. Lobsang Rabgay, 'The Origin and Growth of Medicine in Tibet', in *Tibetan Medicine*, series no. 3, 1994, p. 4.
4. *Ibid.*, p. 5.

the great figures in the Tantro-chemistic field as different from Nāgārjuna, the philosopher. The controversy has not yet been resolved.

Nāgārjuna claimed to be the disciple of Jīvaka, the greatest physician of his times[5] and also the personal physician of Buddha. But this is highly improbable as Nāgārjuna is dated to have lived around 400 years after the Buddha, while Jīvaka was the contemporary of the Buddha. Therefore there must be an interpolation some-where in this lineage.

Jīvaka, around whom many legends had sprung up in his heyday showed remarkable talent even as a young boy. The young prince Jīvaka was the son of Bimbisāra and journeyed all the way to Taxila to study under the celebrated Ātreya. Here he became the object of jealousy on account of his extraordinary brilliance. His competence scaled new heights and he is supposed to have even surpassed his teacher Ātreya twice by correcting him. Among his achieve-ments were the curing of a tumor in the brain of Ajātaśatru for which he adopted a novel method of treatment asking the king to consume the flesh of a young man, and when Ajātaśatru was about to eat, he was so filled with derision that he recalled his parricide and the tumour erupted and disrupted.[6] There is another story of Jīvaka that on observing the footprints of an elephant and the surrounding vegetation, he was able to make a picture that the elephant was blind in one eye and suffered from a host of diseases.[7] The picture surprisingly fitted well.

It is said that all this fame went to his head till he was put in the right place by the Buddha himself. The Buddha lectured to Jīvaka that apart from the physical causes of diseases and their cures, the Four Noble Truths were the four true cures. At that instant, realisation dawned on Jīvaka who understood the phenomena of the reality and then became a monk donning the robes. Accounts of Jīvaka are

5. *Tibetan Medicine,* p. 5.

6. *Ibid.*, p. 12.

7. *Ibid.*

found in the *Vinaya Piṭaka* (ch 23 and 24) and the *Dul- wa Lung shri Sman-shi.* Indian antecedents are remembered well and are regularly referred to in the medical literature. The point of importance is that the same Indian myth like the churning of the ocean was repeated here but recast in a manner showing the Buddha as the source of all knowledge preceding even Brahmā.[8]

The organisational basis of the Buddhist religion paved the way for its development in India and only a few accounts of the history of Tibetan medicine have gone into this aspect. In the Early Pāli canons along with robes, food and lodging, medicine was also included as an essential item of daily need, truly recognising the mental and physical strains the monks had to encounter in their day-to-day life which would place an impediment to their spiritual life.[9] For then without medicine the mind would tend to lose focus on liberation and the prime objectivity would be lost. This was evidently, a take off from the other sects like the Ājivikas, who also had knowledge of the Āyurvedic system then prevalent. The Āyurvedic science of medicine was empirico-rational, that is based on cause effect relationship. Since it were mainly the monks who practised the art of healing, it finally led to the blending of religion and medicine. There is a controversy that the theory of *karma* was incorporated into the medical etiology as it was in tune with the Buddhist view of life world and a factor in the causation of disease. Though if one is tempted to view it as religious superimposition as D.B. Chattopadhyaya says, other like Zysk are disinclined to agree stating that earlier medical theoreticians had accepted it on the level of theory.[10] But it were the early Buddhists who incorporated this spiritual aspect of diseases into their medical etiology. Śākyamuni Buddha was portrayed as a 'miraculous' healer

---

8. Vaidya Bhagwan Dash, 'Āyurveda in Tibet', *The Tibet Journal*, vol. 1 July-September 1975, p. 94.
9. Vinaya Texts, T.W. Rhys Davids and Hermann Oldenberg, tr., rpt., 1965. *Cullavagga*, VI.1.2-VI.2, 2.
10. Kenneth, G. Zysk, *Asceticism and Healing in Ancient India,* 1991, p. 30.

who healed the suffering through psychic or miraculous process and through teaching.[11] The most important achievement of the early Buddhists was that disease was not just viewed as a physical ailment but also a part of the kārmic process which tended to coincide with Buddhist teachings on *karma;* that a person shall beget what he sows. As in daily life the aim of the person was to be liberated from worldly bonds and attain *nirvāṇa* or enlightenment which was the ultimate aim of man according to Buddhist tenets.

The Buddha's method of teaching through parables was well known and examples are legion on how he made people to think and interpret ordinary events in line with his teachings. Death is not final according to the Buddhist theory as the soul reincarnates in another body, the suffering will be more or will be less depending on the *karma* in the earlier birth and disease was another aspect of suffering. So a diseased person was taught to think. There is a story about a person on his deathbed, whose anxious relatives rushed to the Buddha asking him to save the ailing man who was on his deathbed. The Great Master asked the relatives of the patient to get some oil from a household that had never experienced death. The whole exercise came to naught as expected but was overlooked due to belief in magical powers of resuscitating the dead. The Buddha then sermonised to the ailing man about the impermanence of life the process of nature and how futile it was to avoid death as it is an inevitable part of life. There are also many references in the *Vinaya Piṭaka* where the Buddha constantly kept on telling the monks not to forget the Four Noble Truths and he kept on frequently admonishing them whenever they strayed from the path.[12] Often the *bhikkhus* had to face new situations like pestilence when food was not available or at times when meat had to be used as a medicine. The Buddha permitted these practices, strictly keeping the context in mind. It was not prohibited to eat meat but only if the *bhikkhu* had come

11. Raoul Birnbaum, *The Healing Buddha,* 1979, p. 10.

12. *Mahāvagga*,VI.32, 14.

to know that it was not specially slaughtered for him.[13] In other words the motivation to relish meat should be eliminated and it should be viewed as a medicine or food only.

In the *Mahāvagga,* the sixth *Khandaka* is fully devoted to medicaments. Being trained in a philosophical background the monks often contemplated on the root causes of disease in tune with the practice of *dharma.* Significantly Vimalakīrti a *bhikkhu* instructs the *bodhisattva*s to convert the experience of illness into some-thing positive, as illness would not be a hampering factor but rather a catalyst to stimulate renewed dedication for spiritual work.[14] So it can be summarised that the early *bhikkhu*s developed an inclination towards medicine primarily to cure themselves of diseases which acted as impediments in the path of a religious life. Further with the blending of religion and medicine a new explanation arose for the disease, how to cope with it, the role of *karma* and the interlinkages between disease and Karma.

Being recluses, the *bhikkhu*s had no one but only themselves to fall back on and nurse each other. The medical knowledge of the *bhikkhu*s is clearly evident in the *Mahāvagga* where a host of diseases and cures are mentioned and obviously they were in demand by the lay people which is why the Buddha forbid them from practising medicine as it would amount to a professional life. But this advice seems to have been largely disregarded after the Buddha's *parinirvāṇa*, as viewed by some historians.[15]

During the course of their daily wanderings, the *bhikkhu*s encountered practical problems and constantly by methods of debate came to demarcate between medical practices to be followed and those to be abhorred like avoiding flesh or, prohibiting of operations around private parts.[16]

Monasteries also had infirmaries in their precincts and

13. *Mahāvagga*, VI.3214.
14. Raoul Birnbaum, n. 11, p. 12.
15. Raoul Birnbaum, p. 5.
16. *Mahāvagga*, VI.22, 4.

since a good number of monasteries were located on trading routes,[17] it was only logical that they served to the medical needs of the travellers (mostly traders) apart from functioning as rest houses and ports of call providing much needed rest to the weary. This had its economic correlate too, since Buddhism as an institutionalised religion became more and more dependent on the laity for funds therefore it was only natural that they would expect the services of monks in the curative process too.

The development of monasteries into *mahāvihāras* by the seventh century AD is too well known to be recounted here and in these *mahāvihāras* the science of medicine was codified and became part of a well-established curriculum systematically taught as one of the five sciences. Mention may be made here of Taxila which was situated in the north- western part of India and had acquired a high reputation for learning. One of the distinguished products of Taxilā was the famous Jīvaka.

Development of medical education in the monasteries did not follow a linear path throughout the centuries. In fact, interspersed as one system of knowledge is with others and owing to historical changes in the nature of Buddhist religion we may be able to note two significant shifts. One was the development of knowledge in the area concerning the mind of man and its relation with the body which early Buddhism had stressed. In this area the knowledge scaled new heights and a great place was given to mental disorders. Secondly Indian Buddhism itself underwent a metamorphosis incorporating folk beliefs and rituals which were called Tāntric. Here astrology, oracles, astronomy, magical healing, rituals, etc., came into practice as they had popular appeal. All the above-mentioned were incorporated into the medicinal system followed in the monasteries of north India and travelled to Tibet where other developments took place which are detailed in the later part of the chapter.

Among the Indian antecedents which we are looking into,

---

17. Kenneth B. Zysk, n. 10, p. 6.

the period of Buddha is important for the simple reason that the science of medicine came to be imbued with a religious flavour, in this case the Buddhist religion and a philosophical base which was later developed to great heights. The second is the period of the Kāśmīrī physicians Aśvaghoṣa, Janārdana and Candrānanda in the western part of Indian Himālayas, i.e., Kashmir a vibrant source of Buddhist acculturation to Tibet. Aśvaghoṣa, also like Nāgārjuna was a great philosopher but began life as a fervent anti-Buddhist employing his skills in debating to convert the Buddhists. He finally met his match in Āryadeva and became a disciple of Nāgārjuna. Apart from the authorship of the *Jātaka* tales, he is most remembered for his seminal work the *Aṣṭāṅga-hṛdaya-Saṁhitā-nāma,* which the great translator Vairocana was said to have translated with Candrānanda.[18] Candrānanda was a famous disciple of Aśvaghoṣa whose main work is the commentary on the Eight Branches of Medicine.

During the revival of Buddhism in Tibet after Lang-darma's persecution, close contacts developed between western Tibet and Kashmir resulting in many transactions between scholars of an intellectual nature. Translation by Lotsbas was one of the preoccupations of the early Buddhists.

As in the case of script and religion, here also there is a contestation of views that are sufficiently substantive, indicative of the fact that there were Bon medical treatises before the arrival of Buddhism in Tibet. The Bon accounts speak of Lord Shenrab Miwo having taught his son Pyad bu khri-shes the medical text known as *Sman bum dkar nag khra-gsum* and others.[19] The revelation of medical texts by lord Shenrab Miwo bears strong resemblances to Buddhist parallels.

18. *Fundamentals of Tibetan Medicine According to the RGYUD-BZHI*, 1995, p. 2.

19. Dr. Pasang Yonten, 'A History of the Tibetan Medical System', *Tibetan Medicne,* Tsepak Rigzin and Phillipa Russel, tr., series no. 12, 1989, p. 33.

When we stand on firmer historical ground, we get evidences of contacts between Tibetans and neighbouring countries. The historical context at this period shows a picture of Tibet being parcelled into many small princi-palities. This was evidently pre-Buddhist Tibet, and the landmark event in Tibetan medical history was the arrival of two Indian physicians Vijay (Bl-byi-dGah-byed) and Gajay (Be-lha-dGah-mdzes) during the time of LhaTho Tho Ri Nyan Tsen.[20] The physicians from central India became instantly popular and so pleased was the king that he gave his daughter Yid-ki-rol-cha along with a hundred thousand gold coins. The offspring of this couple was the celebrated Dungyi Thorchuk often referred to as the first physician of Tibet. He started a lineage of physicians who were the successive chief royal physicians of the kings.

Great advances were made during the period of Songtsen Gampo, who unified Tibet militarily and politi-cally. His court was adorned with the Indian master physician Bharadvāja, Hen Weng Han the Chinese and Galen the Turkistānī.[21] In addition to their individual works of medical literature, together they composed a volume called *Mi Jigs pa' imtshon cha* which they offered to the king and earned his praise. Galen, the Turkistānī physician was retained at the king's Court and the system of medicine which he followed was called Galenic as in the west or 'The upper or western Tibetan medical system'.[22] This was the period of strong ties with the neighbouring countries, viz., China, India, Nepal and Turkistan, the main areas through which caravans traversed along the silk route.

Turkistan being the westernmost point had many advanced seats of learning with a confluence of scholars from Iraq, Persia and Greece. Thus, it is no wonder that the Galenic system of medicine with its theory of four humors, yellow

---

20. Lady Doctor Lobsang Dolma Khangkar, *Lectures on Tibetan Medicine,* 1989, p. 4.
21. Lobsang Rabgay, n. 3, pp. 18-19.
22. Dr Pasang Yonten, n. 19, p 33.

bile, black bile, phlegm and blood disorders was an exact copy of the Greek system of medicine. In Bon medicine also the theory of four humors was practised giving a lead as to whether Olmo Tagzig the area of its origin may have been the area of the Tājiks which was under Turkic cultural influence. But this is not conclusive and all scholars are not agreed.

The tradition of translation in the Tibetan *gompas* gave a new impetus to the works of medicine also being translated along with the Sūtra and Tantra literature under the aegis of the *gompa*. But this literary activity also had to suffer the partial eclipse during the reign of Langdarma which the Buddhist historians project as a dark period of Tibetan history. Before Langdarma's reign the name of the elder Yuthok Yonthan Gonpo stands out unparalleled in Tibetan medical history and his work is itself a landmark in Tibetan medical history. He was a contemporary of the great Trisong Detsen, one of the patrons of the Buddhist *saṁgha*. At the very young age of 20 the elder Yuthok participated in a medical conference held at Samye, which brought him to the notice of all at large.[23]

Samye, was the first monastery to be built in Tibet and credit for this goes to Śāntirakṣita and Padmasambhava who overcame innumerable odds. Though the duo is famous for the establishment of monasticism on a solid foundation in Tibet, among their achievements was the translation of medical texts having been overshadowed by other greater achievements. The early propagation of Buddhism also led to the spread of medical knowledge to outlying parts of Tibet's areas wherever the *gompa* commanded allegiance. The Four Glorious Tantras of Medicine were the noteworthy translations of the first period. Ācārya Padmasambhava and Trisong Detsen concealed the medicine Tantras in treasure houses, to be discovered later.

Like Yuthok Yonthan Gonpo, other great physicians of his period were Drangti Gyalnye Kharbug, the Court

23. Lady Doctor Lobsang Dolma Khangkar, n. 20, p. 6.

Physician and Nyapa Choeesang. The names of individual physicians like lamas were very important because they formed around themselves a group, which later continued their lineage and preserved their traditions. Most important, as each had contacts with diverse region and practices, new innovations could be brought into practice and systematised rather than there being a single 'frame' of education which would lead to homogeneity disregarding local needs.

The patronage that Buddhism received came to an end during the period of Langdarma when monks had to flee, taking with them their commited group of disciples and practices. Central Tibet was in a state of confusion while the individual efforts at rejuvenating the faith were carried out in other parts, notably in the western Tibetan kingdom of Guge, whose capital Tholing and Purang were centres, where the neighbouring Central Asian cultures inter-mingled. Under the patronage of Yeshe Ö, the great translator Rinchen Zangpo went to India at the early age of 11 and after attaining proficiency in the Sūtras and Tantras initiated a missionary revival, the relics of which are functioning unbroken even today in the *gompas* of Tabo and Alchi which are now only shadows of their past glory. The Lotsba is said to have learnt medicine from the Kāśmīrī physician Janārdana for a sum of a 100 gold coins. It is with the help of Janārdana that Rinchen Zangpo translated the *Aṣṭāṅga-hṛdaya-Saṁhitā-nāma* which is called the Eight Branches, originally authored by Aśvaghoṣa, the Buddhist philosopher whose prolific writings mainly the *Jātaka* tales which are one of the most popular texts have led to writings on medical literature being given a low profile. Rinchen Zangpo also wrote extensive commentaries on the above- mentioned and other works, which served as standard reference material for students of Tibetan and Āyurvedic medicine. By far the name of Vairocana the translator was revered for the translation of the *rGyud-bzhi* or the Four Tantras which was the basis of the Tibetan medical system.[24] And this is said to have happened during the period of king Trisong Detsen when

24. *Fundamentals of Tibetan Medicine*, n. 18, pp. 2-3.

the translator Vairocana is said to have visited India, though there are controversies regarding his visits to India.

The rGyud-bzhi whose complete Sanskrit title is the *Amṛta Hṛdaya Aṣṭāṅga Guhyopadeśa Tantra* Tib: *bDud-rtsi S Nying-po Yan-log Grgya-pa gSang-ba Man-ngag grGyud* ['The Secret Quintessential Instructions on the Eight Branches of the Ambrosia Essence Tantra']. I had earlier mentioned about the lineage of Yuthog Yontan Gompo the Elder (AD 708-833). He shot into prominence after the first international medical conference at Samye, Tibet's first monastery. The rGyud-bzhi is said to have been rewritten at around this time by synthesising from other medical systems like the Galenic, Chinese, etc., which also led to conceptual changes[25] like the concept of Yin and Yang in Chinese medicine, which symbolised cosmic order.

The lineage of Yuthog produced another great name in Yuthog Yontan Gonpo (AD 1126-1202) who is said to have been born as per prophecy. Like his famed predecessor he showed extraordinary talent at a tender age and then went to India. Among his greatest achievements are the redacting of the *rGyud-bzhi* in its present version, in question and answer form which is a bulky work running to 5000 verses all in 156 chapters comprising four texts.[26] From his biography we come to know that he performed many superhuman miracles. He also authored many texts and the lineage continued under his illustrious wards like Sumton Yeshi Zung and the scholar Bumseng. They in turn passed on his teachings to others who belonged to the Drangti lineage.

The Jangpa, Zurkhar and Gongmen traditions are some of the greatest lineages in Tibetan medical history. There is also a story that the son of Galenos founded a lineage called the Lhasa lineage while two of his other sons founded lineages in different parts of the country. It was an inevitable

25. Prof. Samten, G. Karmay, 'Vairocana and the Rgyud-Bzhi', *Tibetan Medicine*, Series no. 12, 1989, pp. 19-24.

26. Dr. Pasang Yonten, n. 22, p. 42.

development as there was no strong central ruler and Tibet was parcelled into many warring principalities. In architecture it mirrors itself in the rise of fortified *gompas* which became competing entities in a power game. So also in the arena of medicine it was the tradition of learning which went from lineage to lineage and the handing down of other things like power, position, knowledge. Till the rise of the reformed sects there was considerable mis-management in the affairs of the *gompa* and localised developments dictated political and day-to-day life, and it was here that the lineages provided the continual links.

The Gelugpa revival and the rise of the institution of the Dalai Lama, who unified vast areas to Tibet, once again brought in new rays of sunshine to the *gompas*. The fifth Dalai Lama, Ngawang Lobsang Gyatso, who took charge of the Tibetan Government (Ganden Phodrang) in 1692 patronised the establishment of three medical centres: Sorig Drophen Ling College, Drang Song Dupsai Lingo College and a school at Lhawang-Chok inside the Potala.[27] Funds were given generously for printing the medical texts and preparation of precious pills. Later the Chakpori medical institute was founded by Desi Sangye Gyatsho in 1696 with support from the fifth Dalai Lama. Chakpori was known[28] for the monumental work done there by Desi Sangye Gyatsho. Here the revival of Tibetan medicine on strong foundation took place with compositions of various texts, the most famous being the treatise on the Four Tantras called *Baidurya Sngon po*. But more importantly at Chakpori the local traditions namely the Jangpa, Zurkhar and the Gongmen were united into one cohesive Tibetan medical system. The last milestone in pre-modern Tibetan medical history was the establishment of the Lhasa Medical and Astro Institute called the Men-Tsee Khang in 1916 on the outskirts of Lhasa.

The purpose of tracing the development of Tibetan

---

27. Dr. Pasang Yonten, n. 22, p. 46.

28. Craig R. Janes, 'The Transformations of Tibetan Medicine', *Medical Anthropology Quarterly*, vol. 9, no.1, March 1995, p. 13.

medicine in a linear chronological perspective is to show how the developments mirrored the political and religious situation. Tibet was open to diverse cultural influences from around and due to such exchanges new medical practices from neighbouring lands notably India, China and the Galenic system from the western borders of Tibet were absorbed, which has been pointed out earlier itself. The high point was the first medical conference at Samye, Tibet's first *gompa.* The post Langdarma period was a period of anarchy. Just as the focus of Buddhist revival shifted to the western part under the patronage of Yeshes' Ö, so too did medical advancement, shift to western Tibet. Rinchen Zangpo the famous translator and central figure in the second propagation of Buddhism translated many medical texts the most famous being the *Aṣṭāṅga-Hṛdaya-Saṁhitā* or *rGyud-bzhi.* Among his protégés the nine physicians of Purang were well known. This phase is in a way very important in the Tibetan medical tradition as the local etiologies developed along with local additions to materia medica. That is why in Tibetan medicine there is difference between the northern and southern tradition which is not very pronounced but any way takes into account local specificities.

The lineages that developed in the different parts of Tibet like the Drangti, Zukhar and Gongmen did a good job by preserving the medical tradition. Among these were a great variety of medical practitioners like famed doctors to village doctors with knowledge of herbal medicines. The famous amongst them were in great demand and transmitted the knowledge to their children and disciples in their private academies, at least two of which were functioning in Tibet (Lhasa and Shigatse). Among the Nyingmapas (who marry) the medical lore is transmitted from father to son while among the Gelugpas, who form the overwhelming majority it is from teacher to pupil. The Chakpori medical college on the outskirts of Lhasa, adjacent to the Potala was the best example of Tibetan medical learning rivalling perhaps only the Men Tsee Khang. Chakpori was in the opinion of Prof. G. Tucci primarily a temple. Most of the teachers were monks, from other *gompas* of Tibet, as also the students and their main clientele were the thousand of monks who lived in the great monastic cities.[29] But smaller *gompas* in outlying areas where there was not a large monastic population catered to the needs of the surrounding villagers and provided them health, services, in addition there was another class of physicians who employed by the government in a full-time or part-time capacity.

Men Tsee Khang was the first non-monastic medical college in Tibet that recruited students from both the monastery, army and aristocratic families. It produced batches of doctors who were placed at monasteries, and government departments. Thus, the institutional phase of development of pre-modern Tibetan medical history ends with the Men Tsee Khang. It is pertinent to note that the Men Tsee Khang did not act as a superordinate or pivotal institution but was only one among a variety of institutions.

Along with the spread of Buddhism to Bhutan, Sikkim, Mongolia and parts of Buryatiya (among the Kalmyks) the Tibetan system of medicine also spread. Here also as in Tibet the standard text was the *rGyud-bzhi*. A point worth noting is that the *rGyud-bzhi* attributed to Bhaiṣajayaguru does not seem to be a literal translation of the original Sanskrit version but is a much more versatile work with Chinese elements, particularly the names of plants but all the properties of such are mentioned according to the Indian *tridoṣa* (three humour) system. In Mongolia, the Tibetan systems of medicine spread like wildfire and the monasteries established there were modelled closely on the Tibetan monasteries and they maintained continuous links with the Tibetan mother monasteries. Here also many students regularly came to Tibet to study in the great monasteries and those with a special aptitude for medicine continued to enroll as students, specialising in medicine as some great lamas did.

In the monasteries a novice entered very early, usually

29. *Medical Anthropology Quarterly*, vol. 9, no.1, March 1995, p. 13.

between the ages of seven and eleven. The first step was mastering the rudiments of Tibetan language, where proficiency in Tibetan language was emphasised. This was because the student should not get confused in reading texts as a single mis-construction of the sentence may change the whole meaning leading to confusion. Stress was on calligraphy, one area where Tibetans demanded a very high standard of accuracy as a single spelling mistake would change the sentence. This was important as the vast materia medica and extensive texts had very subtle differences for similar aspects. Anyway this preliminary training was common for all students wishing to pursue higher studies and only students securing 80 to 90 per cent were given entry for future studies like medicine, astrology, etc.

The whole training course went on for seven long years and was an all round comprehensive course comprising basic menial duties to mechanical memorisation of texts to abstract mental work.[30] First part was spent in the collection of herbs and here the student learn to choose the right type of herb during the right season. The memorisation of the Four Tantras also started during the first year. Everyday during the collection of herbs the teacher tested the students knowledge by asking about the right herbs, flowers, berries, etc., from similar looking ones.

Though examinations both written and oral were held at regular intervals, this type of daily interaction and questioning tested the students knowledge to the limit rather than learning by rote which was the characteristic of other exams. Parallel to this process in the case of monastic education, the day began early for the student at around three in the morning, when the student got up and after the prayers to Manjuśrī, the Buddha of Wisdom there was the memorisation of medical and astrological texts. There-after *haṭha-yoga* was practised by the students. After breakfast at around 8'O clock they offered prayers to their patron deity Sangye Menla the

30. Lady Doctor Lobsang Dolma Khangkar n. 20, p. 20.

Medicine Buddha.[31] Then it was time for individual attention to students depending on their level of understanding. During these seven years the student studied bodily measurements in the afternoon, locating subtle energies as seen in the pulse, analysing the urine, etc. The studies continued till the evening when the students debated on the astrological and medical texts that they had read in the day.[32]

The toughest to master was the pulse diagnosis which would take around seven years to master. During this period other techniques like bloodletting, moxibustion, acupuncture, etc., were taught. The student was allowed to practice along with the doctors only after seven years of study and high premium was placed on his analytical faculties, particularly the analysis of pulse, the records of which were maintained. Only if the student was able to get around 80 per cent of the cases read correctly, was he considered to be fit for medical practice, or he had to go over it for one more year. In some cases it took around thirteen years to complete.[33] Another part of training was the treatment of mental diseases. From the days of early Buddhism, the mind was given a place of prime importance in the scheme of things and the final cure was the taming of the mind. The monastic education laid stress on certain aspects of the mind which were sometimes employed to identify mood disorders and in short help in the functioning of the mind properly.[34]

Like other oriental systems of knowledge, the Tibetan system also subscribed to the view that there is a life energy that moves through the body and when death occurs this energy is said to dissolve, wheras in a state of sickness the energy channels are blocked or disrupted due to disease. The physical manifestations of the disease were variously classified

---

31. Jan Barmark, 'Tibetan Buddhist Medicine from the perspective of the Anthropology ol knowledge', *Tibetan Medicine,* series no. 13, 1991, pp. 3-5.

32. *Ibid.,* p. 6.

33. Lady Doctor Lobsang Dolma Khangkar, n. 20, p. 21.

34. Graham Coleman, ed., *A Handbook of Tibetan Culture*, 1994, rpt., p. 273.

as depression, neurosis, schizophrenia, or in ordinary cases, insomnia, lack of appetite, anxiety. The diseases are given very clear classification which was the basis of the psycho-physical process.[35] Drugs are given for the physical treatment of the disease which can be called the organic process. The most popular was the magico-religious process where cure was done by lamas or unattached lamas (*ngagpa*s) by means of Tāntric and Yogic practices particularly exorcisms, and specific Tāntric rituals like tying of charms to ward off evils, chanting *mantra*s or using geometrical designs which had an abstract meaning symbolising the cosmic order. In the Spiti valley among the Bodhs there is a belief in *Tana-Mana* which literally means magic formulae and when a person is afflicted the qualified lama comes and chants repeating the sacred formula at a ritually prepared altar. Small human and animal figures made of barley flour are prepared and placed over the head of the patient, following which they are thrown on the village crossroads and burnt or buried. During the whole ceremony, several lamas read scriptures.[36] The local people believe that the afflicted spirits are transferred to the images where they will be trapped and after being ritually dismembered they are destroyed not to trouble the person again. Though this had no sanction in the early Buddhist practices it can clearly be noticed that this is a Tāntric practice where local and classical practices of Buddhism were integrated. The third was the practice of *dharma* where the person practices meditation and comes to terms with the reality in accordance with the faith. Tāntric practices are very popular indicative of the fact that the Gelugpa revival which laid stress on the Sūtra could not completely overwhelm the popular mind, accustomed as they were to centuries of 'Shāmanic' beliefs.

This same approach was also found in astrology where

---

35. Dr. Pema Dorji, ed., Jeremy Russell 'Introductory notes on Tibetan Medicine', *Tibetan Medicine,* series no. 12, 1989, pp. 53-62.

36. Srish Jain, 'Traditional Heading and Modern Medical Facilities Among an Indo-Tibetan Community (A brief ethnomedical Survey of the Bodhs of Spiti) *Sman rTsis*, vol. 1, no. 1, 1996, p. 35.

even the nomads and the illiterate villagers knew the name of planets and stars of the constellation of the Bon cosmology but were quite ignorant of Tibetan Buddhist terms for the same.[37] This also goes to show that earlier practices had not been obliterated fully. It can then be surmised that the connection between astrology, astronomy and medicine is not an exclusive Indian import but the interconnections were there earlier too. Anyway our study of Indic sciences would remain incomplete without referring to astrology and astronomy, the allied subjects of medicine.

Along with the founding of the Chakpori medical college the regent of the fifth Dalai Lama, Desi Sangye Gyatso also founded the Astrological and Astronomical department at Chakpori and suggested bringing out an almanac every year in Tibetan,[38] in three versions, extensive for scholars, medium for common people and abridged for the poor and illiterate people. Like medicine, astrology and astronomy in Tibet, Indic sciences were used in day-to-day life. It was not easy to classify these systems of knowledge into watertight compartments in a functional perspective. As the average Tibetan was imbued with a sense of the supernatural he would always seek astrological aid before embarking on any endeavour and in particular before the commencement of any treatment for belief that the correct time will only give the potency of the treatment.

In Tibet there were three systems of astrology namely *kar-tsi* derived from original Sanskrit texts dealing with the movement of planets, *Jung-tsi* based on the five energetical manifestations and translated from Chinese sources and *Yang-char* also derived from Sanskrit texts but kept for long as a secret. *Kar-tsi* is basically astronomy and was called *Kālacakra* Astrology which was said to have been taught by Lord Buddha himself in the eighty-first year of his life. It

37. Dr. Sonam Wangdi and Dr. Philip, 'Astrological Tradition of Tibet part 1 — History' *Tibetan Review*, vol. 14, no. 10, October, 1979, p. 18.

38. Dr. Sonam Wangdi and Dr. Philip, 'Astrological Tradition of Tibet part II — Almanac and Calendar', *Tibetan Review*, vol.14, no.12, December, 1979, p. 8.

was in the year AD 1027 that the *Śrī Kālacakra Tantra* was translated into Tibetan from Sanskrit. Dawa Sangpo the religious king of Shambala was said to have retrieved this system from a south Indian *stūpa*. His son Jampal Dagpo who composed the bsDus-rGyud based on the *Kālacakra* continued this tradition. His son Pema Karpo also wrote an explanatory note entitled *dri-med'od*. His successor Gyal-ka started the practices of the astrological system expounded in the *bsDus-rGyud* and called it *Jyed Tsis*. We further learn that during the time of his successor Nyima the eleventh king of Shambala, *Kālacakra* astrology was brought to India by Dus-Shab Chewa, Tsilu, etc., and then translated and bought lack to Tibet again in the year AD 1027, by Balabodhi Drolo Sherab Dakpa when Tibet was in a state of anarchy.[39] From this long lineage we see that the historicity of the transmission of the text to India and back is rather tenuous and Shambala is yet to be identified. This may be perhaps, to give greater antiquity and acceptance to the text in Tibet as Shambala struck a mystic chord.

It was Desi Sangye Gyatsho who in the year AD 1687 composed the *Baidūrya Kar-po* (White Lapis lazuli) based on the *Pad dkar Zhal-Ling* and distributed his work during an annual *Monlam* festival, subsequently challenging anyone to compose either a beginning or an end to it. Though he was the head of the state, two people Lochen Dhama Shri of Orgyan Mindroling the famous astrological school near Lhasa and Phyong Gyaspa Ngawang made critical studies which were then incorporated into it, as a follow up entitled *Bai durya gYa-sel*.[40] This only goes to show that as in the tradition of philosophical debate where rival parties would sit and debate, free from pressures of power and the likes of it, in an open audience. The same spirit of debate was evident even in technical fields also. This was because when it came to debate the autonomy of the subject mattered and in full view the public could not always be made to acquiesce in favour of any one party, but rather use their own judgement.

39. Dr. Sonam Wangdi and Dr. Philip, n. 37, p. 18.

40. *Ibid.*, n. 37, p. 19.

There are many tales in Tibet of the high and mighty, having been made to see the other point of view.

When it came to the day-to-day usage, the first chapter of the *Kar-tsi* dealing with the cosmology and the movement of stars formed the basis for the Tibetan almanac and calendar of which there were three versions, the extensive for the astrologer, the medium for the common people and an abridged version for the overbusy or illiterate folk.[41] The second chapter dealt with the *cakra*s or energy centres of the body and the effects that the external planets have on these centres which in turn lead to effect on bodily organs and mood variations. The third and final chapter was the alternative *kālacakra* and was most important for meditation and also followed as a technique in Yogic practices where one visualised one *yidam* or personal deity.[42] Certain features of astronomy like the eclipse were explained as the coming of earth in between of the sun and the moon which is akin to the modern concepts. This was a departure from the traditional Hindu notion of an eclipse wherein Rāhu, the shadowy planet swallows the moon. In addition there was also a monthly almanac called *zla tho* which was mainly used in the calculation of agricultural cycles of sowing and also disposal of dead bodies.[43]

The second system called *Jhung-tsi* and was said to have originated from China and was said to have been brought to Tibet during the reign of Nyatri Tsenpo and translated thrice during the reigns of Namri Songtsen, Songtsen Gampo and Trisong Detsen. During the rule of the last mentioned many students were sent to China to learn this system.[44] It was not entirely a Chinese system as is evident from the fact that in *Jhung-tsi* calculations, there are the five elements, twelve

---

41. Dr. Sonam Wangdi and Dr. Philip, n. 38, p. 8.
42. Prof. Jampa G. Dagthon 'An Introduction to Tibetan Astro Science' in Jhampa Kalsang, tr., *Tibetan Astronomy and Astrology — A brief introduciton,* 1995, p. 17.
43. Charles Bell, *The People of Tibet,* 1991, rpt., pp. 43-7.
44. Dr. Sonam Wangdi and Dr. Philip, n. 37, p. 19.

animal signs, nine magic square numbers (*sMewa*) and the eight *parkhas* or trigrams which were arranged in a circle around the *sMewa* in an astrological chart. Earlier Bon astrological system had already been using the five elements. It is the system of eight *parkhas* or trigrams each symbolising a personal deity that comes from China. From China the principle of *Yin* and *Yang*, the binary opposites also are used in this system.

This system formed the basis for the *rapchung* or sixty-year cycle into which the Tibetan calendar is divided. Each year is a combination of an element from amongst the five elements and an animal from among the twelve animals. This calculation is used in day-to-day life to find out about Srog or life energy, Lus or health condition, Wangthang — financial situation and rLung tha or success. Most of the problems stemmed from imbalance of energy, or effects of evil spirits. The spirits were then placated by *pūjās* or giving alms. Also before applying moxibustion and blood letting, a doctor had to determine the seat of the patients vital energy. This was important as seasonal influences lead to variations in the pulse, and pulse reading is one of the most important parts in the analysis of disease.[45] Medicines were to be manufactured, collected and the raw materials sourced only at the appropriate months and seasons as this was believed to have special properties. Herbal plants were to be collected in spring, medicinal flowers in summer, fruits and berries of medicinal value in autumn, etc. It was then determined by astrology at which particular phase of the season must the items be collected as the potency reached its peak at that phase.[46]

The next system is called *Yangchar* which was also derived from Sanskrit texts but was for long kept a secret and

---

45. Jampa Gyaltsen Dagthon 'Astrology and the Tibetan Art of Healing' tr. and annotated by Tashi Tsering and Glenn H. Mullin, *Tibetan Review,* vol. 1, Feb-March 1980, p. 12.

46. *Ibid.,* p. 13.

transmitted orally as many other esoteric doctrines.[47] The *Yangchar* is called, the arising from the vowel system and here the logic is that all planets exert some influence on a person and depending on the plarticular time and phase through which he is passing the planetary positions and their influences can be predicted. During the individuals life he will be always influenced by the nine planets and a bad phase means that he is influenced by either Sun, Mars, Rāhu, Saturn and Ketu which are supposed to be violent planets. Moon is a peaceful planet and during its ascendancy the person will enjoy good success, prosperity and sound sleep.

But there arose moments in an individuals life when even the best medicine could not cure him and he is almost given up for dead. In such cases the astrologer suggested a last ditch effort where an effigy of the person was made and then offered to the evil spirits which were believed to encircle it. This ritual called *gto* was performed only in times of extreme helplessness.[48] A similar variant is found in the Spiti valley called *rolance*. Here a person's effigy is made and a mock funeral is enacted. While the pallbearers call out and proclaim that the person is dead to confuse the evil spirits.[49] Both these are believed to be a carry over from pre-Buddhist Bon traditions.

Apart from medicine, astrology was used as a guiding factor right from the day a child was born, from the casting of the horoscope, to illness, marriage, journeys, new ventures and death ceremonies or even in ordinary moments of anxiety. So the role of the astro practitioner was a daily part of the Tibetans life.

Another system of predicting the future was by divination using beads, dice and even doughball.[50] Divination

47. Jhampa Kalsang, Tsipa Kachupa, 'Traditional Community Role of the Astro Practitioner', *Tibetan Astronomy and Astrology — A brief Introduction*, 1995, p. 23.
48. Professsor Jampa G. Dagthon, n. 43, p. 14.
49. Sirish Jain, n. 36, p. 35.
50. 'Divination in Tibet', *Choyang,* no. 6, 1994, p. 112.

was resorted to in cases of choice where one had to make a decision. In monasteries questions of leadership and hierarchical problems were settled by doughball divinations, where slips of paper were put inside doughballs and worshipped for two to three days after which the doughball was taken and the slip inside was the final result. Divination helped to overcome anxiety and above all made the person rationalise his choice, as the future course was unknown thereby eliminating conflict which would other- wise act as a drag on the motivation. In case of rosary and dice divination results of three chances were taken which only helped to confirm that the outcome was not pure chance but an extension or the way to be followed. Shoulder blade divination was especially popular among the nomads. The doughball divination was a time taking procedure but the prayers gave an element of sanction to the whole process and a divine element is involved in the choice which would otherwise have led to conflicting opinions promoting discord.

In the study and practice of astrology and astronomy, there was no need to refer to medical texts but for the medical science it was absolutely essential to study and rely upon a knowledge of astrology. From an empirico-rational viewpoint the blending of astrology with medical science sounds rational but when we take man's personality into account which according to philosophical anthropologists, he lives in three worlds, his inner mental world, his life world and others. This is in direct contrast to Western empirical science that sees man primarily in a biological framework. In Tibetan medicine the three worlds are indivisible and united, therefore sharp distinctions were not made between the physical health and spiritual life. One of the historical causes for this was the great body of knowledge in Buddhist religion, about the inner world of man. The primary aim of Buddhism to understand the mental process and transform them, i.e., 'taming the mind'.

Conclusion

Tibetan medicine, astronomy and astrology flowered under

the patronage of the monastery. Together they are called Indic sciences, as the main theoretical orientation went from the advanced Indian systems of *Āyurveda*, astronomy, and astrology. Medicne in particular exhibited a striking correlationship in its attainments with the varying position of the *gompa*. It was originally introduced from the famed *mahāvihāra*s of India (Pāla and north-western India). It suffered a temporary eclipse during the aftermath of the post Langdarma period. Later period saw the rise of lineages like Jangpa, Drungti, Yuthok which kept the tradition alive, finally reaching a high level during the reign of the fifth Dalai Lama with the founding of the Chakpori Medical College. Medicinal theories were also borrowed from China, and Central Asia along with early Tibetan practices which were synthesised in the Āyurvedic theory. Development of medicine, schooling and training of doctors followed a strict Tibetan Buddhist pattern by emphasising the need for compassion and also integrating the mystic element in the form of rituals like *gto,* concept of Bardo.

Similarly astrology and astronomy reached their peak during the fifth Dalai Lama's period with the founding of the Chakpori, where an academy was started for this purpose. This period was crucial as all the major traditions were unified into a national style similar to the emergence of a national style in painting. Medicine, astronomy and astrology have strong interrelationships, as the concept of an auspicious time emerged, which deemed that any act had to be undertaken at an auspicious time for efficacy determined by astrology. Monks thus helped the lay people by treating them and also in overcoming their predicaments. Schooling of the *amchi*s was standardised with an extensive materia medica and technical development in medicine like blood letting, moxibustion and acupuncture.

Likewise, astrology and divination played a solacing role for the common man when he undertook any venture. Thus, the development of Indic sciences led to the integration of *gompa* with the community.

3

Monastic Organisation and Education

GOMPAS established in Tibet were modelled on the famous *mahāvihāra*s (monastic universities) of India namely Oḍantapurī, Vikramaśilā, Oḍḍiyāna, Nālandā, etc. From the days of early Buddhism, i.e., from the time of Śākyamuni Buddha, one of the major factors leading to a change in the organisational structure of monasticism was education. There are many references in the *Vinaya Piṭaka* to bands of recluse *bhikkhu*s under the leadership of a senior *bhikkhu* doing the rounds and collecting alms. During their daily social dealings they had to come face to face with the brāhmaṇas who considered them as heretical, and disputes broke out on matters of philosophy and religion. So the *bhikkhu*s united themselves under a senior *bhikkhu* who would provide the intellectual leadership as unity was the need of the hour; this was one of the practical needs for having a learned person as a head who could outdo others in debates. Further, a knowledgeable person was a *śramaṇa,*[1] who was respected in the social circle at par with a brāhmaṇa, the former because of his intellectual achievements and the latter due to his birth. Śākyamuni Buddha was himself referred to as a *śramaṇa.*[2]

Above all the cardinal pillar on which Buddhism is founded are the 'Four Noble Truths' which conclude that ignorance is the root cause of all misery and suffering; therefore the only way to attain liberation was through a

1. R.S. Sharma, *Material Culture and Social Formations in Ancient India*, 1992, rpt. pp. 120-131.
2. *Vinaya Texts, The Cullavagga,* VII.3, 7.

thorough understanding of the working of the world which was blurred by ignorance. Knowledge was the redeemer of man and it is no wonder that, since the days of the early Buddhists, such an exalted place was given to this faculty of human action.

The prevalent system of education in Ancient India was the *guru-śiṣya paramparā* or the teacher-student tradition where the student, a celibate (*brahmacārin*) stayed at the residence of the teacher, and acquired knowledge in the sacred lore which was the major area of study though other subjects were also taught. The development of the *saṁgha* led to an organised body of officials whose main pursuits apart from the enforcement of rules and religion were connected to knowledge. According to the Pāli *Mahāvagga,* there were two categories of preceptors for a novice who entered the *saṁgha*, the *upajjhaya*s who looked after the spiritual upliftment and taught the novice the moral rules of conduct, and an *ācārya* or teacher who taught the spiritual texts and looked after the educational progress of the person.[3] Like the *guru-śiṣya paramparā*, the relationship was replicated here and the novice had to do work for the monastery as servants were not allowed to enter the monastery.

By the end of the Gupta period, development of trade led to mercantile patronage along with royal patronage making monasteries wedded to the single pursuit of learning. The most famous among these were the celebrated *mahāvihāra*s, which had many colleges, hostels and libraries, like the Nalanda University under the celebrated Śīlabhadra as its head which had its own seal that read *nālandā-mahā-vihārīya-ārya-bhikṣu-saṁghasya*[4] attracting students from Sri Lanka, Malaya, Burma (Myanmar), Indonesia, Tibet and other countries. There were separate hostels for foreign students. In addition to the monks, laypersons were also

3. S. Dutt, 'Buddhist Education' in P.V. Bapat, ed., *2500 Years of Buddhism*, 1997, 6th rpt., p. 158.

4. Sukumar Dutt, *Buddhist Monks and Monasteries of India*, 1962, p. 336.

taught; teachers being famous monks and both sacred and secular subjects were taught like building, engineering.[5] Huien Tsang[6] has given a good description of Nalanda University and around the same time Thonmi Sambotha, the celebrated Tibetan scholar came to India at the instance of the great Songtsen Gampo and is credited with introducing a script for the Tibetans, the Lentsa a modified version of the then existing Indian Gaṇḍi script suitably modified to Tibetan phonetics.[7] Though this is a matter of controversy as recent historical research has questioned this assumption. The Samye monastery, the first in Tibet was modelled on the fabled Oḍantapurī monastery. Thus, the monastic model which Tibet inherited was fully based on the multifunctional *mahāvihāra.* This process continued and new monasteries sprang up all over Tibet, thanks to the munificence of the able successors of Songtsen Gampo particularly Trisong Detsen and Ralpachen. The religious texts have over-emphasised the role of the early religious kings Songtsen Gampo, Trisong Detsen and Ralpachen who constructed only thirteen monasteries in the whole of Tibet. It was after Langdarma's persecution of Buddhism that we see the unleasing of the pent up energies of the Buddhist missionaries which was on a larger scale, far more than the Chogyal period.[8] The breaking point came in with the enthronement of Langdarma who disrupted the monasteries forcing the monks to flee. Tibet was not to be a united nation any longer.[9] The Buddhist revival started from Tholing, the capital of the western Tibetan kingdom of Guge under the patronage of Yeshes Ö[10] whose protégé, the famous Rinchen Zangpo, translator and builder of monasteries heralded the Buddhist revival. Rinchen Zangpo is credited with the founding of

---

5 *Buddhist Monks and Monasteries of India,* p. 333.

6. *Ibid.,* p. 332.

7. *The Blue Annals,* (Part One), George N. Roerich, tr., 1949, p. 39.

8. Dawa Norbu, *Tibet The Road Ahead*, 1997, pp. 368-9.

9. *The Blue Annals,* p. 60.

10. *Ibid.,* p. 68.

hundred and eight monasteries in the western Himālayas. The number hundred and eight is a conventional number and therefore must be properly accompanied by facts. But there is no doubt that Lotsba Rinchen Zangpo established a number of monasteries. Some of them survive even today. Among them are Tabo, Alchi, Kanum which have the appendage Chos-khor attached to them which means a doctrinal complex, i.e., a centre for theological studies. This was the institutional organisation of Buddhism which Tibet inherited from India and two benefits accrued to the Tibetans from the outset. First, they did not have to go through an evolutionary process of the development of the *saṁgha* stage by stage as in India and secondly, the first generation of Tibetan Buddhists who had studied in India were acquainted with the management and establishment of large monasteries.

The recruits to the monastery entered at a rather young age of seven and then they progressed further as in normal educational institutions advancing further up the grade after every stage of examination. Though it was not necessary that a recruit enter at the specified age (he may even enter at the age of 40 as there have been some cases) but the ages of seven to eleven were generally followed. All sections of the society were eligible to enter the Order but in Tibet, was followed the policy that blacksmiths and butchers were denied entry on the ground that the former manufactured iron weapons that were used in the taking of life and the latter's profession essentially demanded the slaying of animals both of which were in direct contravention of the Buddhist policy of non-violence.[11]

The first step for the laity/boy to enter the monastery was to find a sponsor who would vouch for his discipline and overall behaviour in the monasteries. Usually it was a close relative in the monastery, mostly uncles who under-took to sponsor the boy. This was so as each village had its own *gompa,* which was in turn affiliated to a mother *gompa.* It

11. Giuseppe Tucci, *Tibet: Land of Snows,* J.E. Stapleton Driver, tr., 1967, rpt., p. 93.

was logical that the recruit would go to the *gompa* to which his village was associated as this *gompa* had many socio-economic links with the village.

Normally a child stayed at home till the age of eight and was first a pupil probationer (*da-pa*), then a novice (*getsul*) and finally a fully ordained monk (*gelong*). The boys were examined for any physical defect like a squint eye, harelip, or any anatomical disorders, that would stand in the way of the normal discharge of duties. The parentage of the boy was enquired into and in some *gompa*s, preference for aristocracy was shown, though this was only a later development.[12] The first stage was a preparatory schooling for entering into the noviciate and there were not many rituals and ceremonies to mark the occasion. The relative of the boy in the monastery took care of him while there was a tutor or elder to coach the boy as there were no fixed classes. It was the tutor who led the boy to the gathering of the monks in the hall, where the presents *Chang* (beer), money and eatables, were offered, followed by a small statement declaring publicly the boy's lineage, and on getting an affirmation from the elder monks (*dg-u-chas*) the boy became a pupil probationer. Thus started the formal education of the boy beginning with the rudiments of the Tibetan language and then proceeding on to learn the sacred books of Padma-sambhava, dealing with sacrifice, wisdom, etc., all of which were concise and held in high esteem.[13] Another type of education was through the teaching of maxims and proverbs, which was popular even during the lifetime of the Buddha.[14] These touched mostly upon the moral and behavioural aspects and metaphorically explained in brief an idealised set of behavioural codes. For example, they were given four principles of speech and it was said, 'if the speech is too long it is tedious, if it is too short its meaning is not appreciated, if

---

12. L.A. Wadell, *Buddhism and Lamaism of Tibet,* 1974, rpt., p. 174.
13. *Ibid.,* pp. 173-7.
14. *Vinaya Texts, The Mahāvagga*, V.1.16.

rough it ruffles the temper of the hearers, if soft it is unsatisfying'. The initial period lasted for around two to three years and was mainly a period when the pupil got acclimatised to the monastic environment and only the very obstinate were weeded out. Apart from this, a considerable time of the *ge-tsul* was spent in serving the senior monks by way of doing menial duties. This practice was adopted during the period of the *saṁgha*'s genesis and had stayed on. Even in the early days of Buddhism we hear of different positions held by the monks. Though the local people were employed in menial activities (mostly agricultural) on the premises of the *gompa,* they were not permitted to enter the hall and serve the monks; rather, their presents were to be left at the doorstep of the monasteries from wherein the respective *getsul*s did the service.

The next stage was that of the novice when the actual process of induction into monastic life began. By now the candidate would have memorised the necessary texts after which his tutor lama applied to the head monk (*Spyi-rgan*) for permission to admit the applicant and then sealing the agreement with a silk scarf (*lha-rdsas*) and a token sum of money. The next procedure was to go to the abbot (*khenpo*) of the particular school in the monastery and seek to register the name of the pupil who was escorted now along with his tutor who made an offering of a scarf and a silver coin and bowed before him. In big monasteries there was a three-tier organisation consisting of La-chi (the University board), Dra Tshang (the college) and Khamstsen (a type of dormitory or residential quarters). The Dra Tshang was the most important unit which was administered by a Khenpo and had a high degree of autonomy in the say of syllabus,[15] discipline, rules besides power over its own property and real estate. Thus, it goes to say that considerable autonomy was there particularly in the field of syllabus and teaching procedure that gave an important space for innovation, though most literature on *gompa* do not highlight this fact

---

15. Kunchok Sithar, 'Tibetan Monastic Life in the Past and Present', *Tibetan Review*, vol. 24, March 1989, pp. 11-12.

but rather present the whole programme as a rigid scholastic one which appears to be dreary.[16]

Finally, after getting the nod from the Khenpo, the boy was asked some questions as to whether he came on his own free will or not? Was he a debtor, slave or was he free from contagious disease or deformity, or had he neglected the three vows, took any life and details about his family? The first point that whether the boy came of his own free will has aroused considerable debate and many are of the opinion that at such a young age it was beyond the capacity of the boy to take such a major decision of his future life and that this was just a mere formality. It cannot be denied that due to customary and socio-economic reasons many parents admit their wards to the monastery. Far from seeing this situation from an ethnocentric perspective, the objective reality in pre-modern Tibet was that of a society imbued with a high sense of religiosity. In such a setting a very large percentage of people became monks (all historians do not agree on the percentage monks though estimates vary, from 13 to 25 per cent).[17] It can be said that the prevalent ideology aimed at the constant procurement/recruitment of monks in the hope that the ultimate aim of man was to get salvation both individually and collectively and monasticism was the best way out. In such a value system it was not strange that such values got internalised as the whole person of the monk was respected. Regarding debtors and slaves, Śākyamuni had disallowed them entry into the monastery as their motives were mercenary, though some modern historians state that it was in support of retaining the system which would benefit the slave owners. The question relating to neglect of the three commandments, taking of lives were viewed seriously as the person lacked conviction.

After getting a satisfactory reply, the pupil was examined in the texts that he had learnt and had to recite it by heart. Should he fail in any of these, not only did he get rejected

16. Giuseppe Tucci, n. 11, p. 93.

17. Geoffrey Samuel, *Civilized Shamans Buddhism in Tibetan Societies,* 1993, pp. 578-82.

from the monastery, but his tutor also suffered shame and the pupil, a few strokes of the cane. For the successful candidate, a ceremony awaited and he was brought bedecked in all his regal finery that he would be wearing for the last time in his life. After some time this would be exchanged for the robes of the monastery exactly in the same way as the Buddha discarded all his regalia symbolising the renunciation of all worldly ties. Now the novice, called *da-pa* has his head shaved and finally became a member of the monastery though not fully entitled to all the privileges. His daily education was mixed with a judicious blend of discipline, a shrewd dose of psychology and occasional punishments that could even amount to caning. The *da-pa* was by now well acquainted with the etiquette of the monastery and apart from studying, a greater part of the day was spent in doing some assigned duties. The examinations were held regularly, the first within a year and next after the second or third year. After clearing these examinations the *da-pa* could get a small chamber in his Khamtsen. After some more exams he was spared of the menial duties.

The examination itself was a display of one's memory and knowledge in public lasting for around three days, and nine intervals were allowed during the examination. Though most of the students failed in the first attempt the great majority passed in the second attempt while repeated failure for three years lead to the candidate getting rejected from the monastery. The failure of the boy was reflected on the teacher also and if the boy failed the teacher was chastised but on his good performance the teacher got accolades. According to Tucci,

> the examination system is arranged so judiciously and the rites accompanying it are so magnificent that the neophyte is overawed and seeks for himself a place in the hierarchy.[18]

---

18. Giuseppe Tucci, n. 11, p. 68.

Tucci's contention is based on the fact that at the moment there occurs a metamorphosis of mind and soul, which leads the neophyte to seek a rank in the hierarchy. We may accept this contention but it can also be pointed out that having got to know of the monastic life by experiencing it as a student, menial, 'alternate family', i.e., in various capacities, judgement of all the neophytes would not be one of getting overwhelmed.

The whole course was of twelve years though it varied in different Orders and also in monasteries. By the time a man was fully ordained as a monk (*gelong*) he completed twelve years of education. The final stage of education was the *Geshe* degree and was a very respectable one. For further study in specialised colleges of esoteric earning, a *Geshe* degree was must. The *Geshe* degree was originally started by the Śākya tradition and was called *ka-chi* (four subjects) or *ka-ju* (ten subjects). For the *Geshe* degree, the curriculum was divided into six main subjects which were organised into fifteen classes. There were collected topics (*Godus-gra*) which were preliminary to the syllabus proper.

- Perfection of wisdom (Prajñāpāramita, *phar-yin*)
- Middle View (Mādhyamika, *dbuma*)
- Valid Cognition (Pramāṇa, *tshadma*)
- Discipline (Vinaya, *Dul-ba*)
- Knowledge (Abhidharma, *mzod*)[19]

As stated earlier the number of years a candidate spent varied from college to college but it was more or less in this way:

Collected topics, one year
Perfection of wisdom, five years
Middle view, two years
Discipline, one year
Knowledge, two years

---

19. 'The *Geshe* Degree', *Choyang*, no. 3, 1993, p. 102.

> Valid cognition was studied intermittently throughout the course.[20]

As a carryover from the fabled Indian monasteries of Pāla India where Tibetan presence was already two centuries old, the systems of knowledge in Tibet also followed Indian patterns of organisation into ten categories, five major and five minor; these are given below with their Sanskrit and English equivalents.

Five Major Fields

Tibetan	***Sanskrit***	***English***
Bzo-rig-pa	*Śilpa-Śāstra*	Technology
Gso-ba-rig-pa	*Cikitsā-Śāstra*	Medicine
Rgrai-rig-pa	*Śabda-Śāstra*	Grammar
Tshod-ma-rig-pa	*Pramāṇa-Śāstra*	Logic
Nang-don-rig-pa	*Dharma-Śāstra*	Religion

Five Minor Fields

Tibetan	***Sanskrit***	***English***
Snran dngags	*Kāvya-Śāstra*	Poetics
Sdeb sbyor	*Chanda-Śāstra*	Metrics
Mngon brojd	*Abhidhāna-Śāstra*	Lexicon
Zlos gor	*Nāṭya-Śāstra*	Dramatics
Rtsis	*Jyotiṣa-Śāstra*	Astrology

Some *gompas* were famous for a particular branch of study as Chakpori for medicine (which was primarily a temple), Narthang, famous for printing. Besides, the students were free to practice the field of knowledge depending on their aptitude and inclination, as some students preferred Tāntric studies, etc. The fact that the syllabus was considerably modified under each teacher allowed for innovation. Another point which mitigates against the grains of rigidity was specialisation. Big physical distances were not

20. 'The *Geshe* Degree', *Choyang*.

an obstacle to study at a particular *gompa* famed for its excellence like Drepung, Sera and Ganden which attracted talent from as far as Mongolia and Bhutan.[21]

The Gelugpas' attached great importance to these open debates. In a popular form of debate, there was one challenged person who defended a question against any number of challengers.

For the *Geshe* examination, the candidate had to face the General debate which was a very pompous occasion, and preceded by exhibitory debates in the college. For this he took permission from his college study supervisor (*lama shung leg-pa*) and asked him to recommend a subject to comment and on the appointed day in all royalty, the *lama* took his seat on a throne and the candidate prostrated before him. All were fed a meal and then the debate started with the verses given to the *Geshe* candidate by the *lama shung leg-pa*. The most important debate was the all night debate on the topic of valid cognition, which took place at the winter congregation at Tang. What made this debate livelier was that all the challengers were advanced debaters. The *Geshe*s were awarded their degrees at the twenty-fourth of the first month at the end of the Great Prayer Festival (*Monlam Chenmo*). If the Dalai Lama was at Lhasa, he personally presided over the event, which took place in the upper story of the Jokhang temple, eagerly watched by the members of the colleges to which the candidates belonged and eagerly waiting to know who topped with the highest ranks. The *Geshe*s were called out by name by a government official and presented dry fruits and a robe.

With regard to the *Geshe* examination, it may be pointed out that this was also a costly affair as the *Geshe* candidate had to give gifts and meals to his whole college and other officials which placed a considerable strain on his purse. It was one of the reasons why many of the candidates who had completed their studies did not go in for the *Geshe* degree.

---

21. Kalden T. Lodro and Jermey Rusell, 'Namgyal Monastery', *Choyang*, no. 3, 1993, pp. 5-6.

The process of giving gifts was a custom right from the time the candidate entered the monastery. When the noviciate failed repeatedly and was subject to removal from the monastery, he could be readmitted again on giving gifts which were much higher in value than he had given earlier. In some monasteries of Sikkim there was a marked preference for Tibetans of pure descent and so was the case in Lahaul and Spiti, where the famed monasteries of Kadrang in Lahaul, Ridzong in Ladakh were attracting elite Gelugpa families.[22] Similarly, the *Geshe* degree itsell was a point of controversy and was a subject of reform when the thirteenth Dalai Lama started his reforms. Originally established in the Gelugpa Order formally, at the time of the fifth Dalai Lama the *Geshe* degree was awarded to some old monks first on the basis of seniority, thereby diluting the standards. On a tour to Mongolia the debating skills of the local Mongolian scholars impressed the thirteenth Dalai Lama so much that he then instituted reforms that the degree of *Geshe* be given only to candidates who had really proved their worth in all the educational and debating skills, i.e., in all the aspects of what was originally expected of a candidate.[23] In the ritual, prior to the college exhibitory debate, the *Geshe* candidate had to offer a meal to the rest of his college and immediately prior to the meal, the head of the hostel led him and he circled the monks holding a stick of incense and a banner on which were inscribed some verses. Originally the verses were composed by the *Geshe* candidate himself to demonstrate his erudition, but in course of time things came to such a pass that any auspicious verse would do. This showed the level of formality ascribed to rituals which originally had been devised with a purpose in mind that, in this case, was a creative one.

The degree of *Geshe Lha Rampa* was not the highest degree and there was an advanced degree, that of *Rab Jam-pa* which was compared to that of the Doctor of Theology. These degrees like that of the *Geshe* degree were a still more

---

22. O.C. Handa, *Buddhist Monasteries in Himachal Pradesh*, 1987, p. 122.

23. 'The *Geshe* Degree', n. 20, p. 104.

expensive affair and the whole doctrine, Buddhist church and faith were the topics for public disputation to get this prestigious degree. The honour accorded to this degree could be gauged from the fact that the holder of a *Rab Jam-pa* degree was entitled to wear a special hat, which was regarded as a sign of an exalted status. In the Lamaist hierarchy, the hats and other accompaniments like cowl were the markers of status and achievement that distinguished between the ordinary lamas and those high up in the hierarchy. A *Rab Jam-pa* could teach the Buddhist Law in public and was chosen for the highest posts in the monastic hierarchy except those positions that were reserved for the incarnate lamas. In addition to this, there were the titles of *Cho-je* and *paṇḍita* which meant 'Noble of the Law' and 'Learned' respectively, which are not degrees but titles of such honorific value and were bestowed only upon those *Geshe*s who had proved their worth by an excellent display of wisdom and who were also of blameless character; that is a person who had earned a name not only by erudition but also by his deeds. The most famous *paṇḍita* in the Tibetan history was the Śākya *paṇḍita* whose exposition of Buddhist faith and force of personality transformed the rugged Mongols who till then were a terror in Central Asia to one of the gentlest people on the earth.[24] Another famous title was that of *Lotsba* which was a step lower than that of the *paṇḍita*. *Lotsba* literally means 'translator' and since the days of *Lotsba* Rinchen Zangpo, translators have been held in high esteem in Tibet as the great corpus of Sanskrit, Pāli and Chinese Buddhist literature, but predominantly Sanskrit literature along with an almost large number of secular works in Sanskrit were being constantly translated, and also commentaries on many works were being translated.[25]

After a candidate passess the *Geshe* degree, the options open to him for further studies were to study at the two Tāntric colleges Gyuto or Gyumey. This was also part of the reforms

---

24. Tsepon, W.D. Shakabpa, *Tibet — A Political History*, 1998, p. 68.
25. *The Blue Annals*, n. 7, pp. 102-7.

of the thirteenth Dalai Lama who had made it compulsory for *Geshes* to study at these Tāntric institutions to raise the standard of education in the Tāntric colleges and also to complete their education with a thorough study of the Tāntras.[26] The reformed sects had always stressed on the primacy of the Sūtra or the original teaching of the Buddha over the Tantra, but with such a mass appeal it was not possible to completely relegate the Tāntric system to the background. This probably was the reason for the Gelugpa's to insist on the study of the Tantra, i.e., the esoteric after already finishing the exoteric studies, as the esoteric element had always been popular in Tibetan Buddhism. The education at these two academies laid great stress on Yoga and meditation, the former was believed to elevate the adherent to a higher state of physical spiritual field and meditation which was to control the mind. The training was based on a unique master pupil relationship and the pupil picked up a personal god as his ideal and remodelled his personality to attain union with him. For this purpose, many rituals and aids were used; the ultimate aim being to attain unity of the finite, i.e., of the individual self with the infinite (universal self[27]). The Dalai Lama personally selected the graduates of these academies for teaching posts in these institutions. These were not the only academies but there were many Tāntric monasteries and nunneries where stress was laid on Yoga and Tāntric texts and meditation and most importantly their application. Though the *Geshe* degree was open only to monks, nuns also had degrees that were less comprehensive.[28] Though it sounds indicative of an inferior status for nuns, it was a fact that women teachers could also teach monks as well as nuns.[29] Also, in the highest form of esoteric study, a monk or

---

26. Sherpa Tulku, Khamlung Tulku, Alexander Berzin and Jonathan Landaw, 'The Structure of the Gelug Monastic Order', *The Tibet Journal*, vol. 23, no. 3, Autumn, 1998, pp. 67-9.
27. *The Blue Annals,* pp. 118-19.
28. Franz Michael, *Rule by Incarnation: Tibetan Buddhism and its Role in Society and State,* 1982, p. 167.
29. *Ibid.*

nun could retire to isolated temples or caves for short or long periods and then preach to their followers with the insight they had gained through this advanced exercise. A very good example of this aspect is of the *yogīs* of Śilā[30] in the remote Zanskar valley belonging to the sTagrimo Gompa affiliated to the Dukpa Kagyu Order and retired to the hills of Śilā for advanced esoteric meditation and training. The main focus of training after the preliminaries was on contemplation and lasted for a total of twenty-seven months, the whole schedule remaining unchanged for centuries.

The above description is a short account of the religious education of the Gelugpa School. In addition to that, we have the other orders and also the secular education as monks performed a host of duties in the government, in their official capacities. Among the Nyingmapas great stress was laid on the magical rites and Yoga as they believed that the Inner Light of man could be best revealed by the Tāntric and Yogic exercises which were called *dzogchen.* The Bonpo and Nyingmapa shared striking similarities, like non-celibate monasticism, being less centralised and hierarchical, and emphasis on Tāntric practice in general. The *dzogchen* tradition is common to both these sects, though technically speaking, the Bonpos are not Buddhists but from a division of monastic and sectarian typology they can be regarded as a Buddhist Order. Like the Nyingmapas, the Kagyu-pas who trace their origin from Marpa also laid emphasis on the mystical element and here they borrowed heavily from the Indian *siddhas* like Tilopa and Naropa. Their basic aim is like the Nyingmapas, i.e., to transcend the temporal existence and achieve union with the ultimate self, to achieve which they used *haṭhayogic* techniques of breath control and exercises, which lead to a state of ecstasy. It was this state of ecstasy which the Kagyupa's believed that led one to Buddhahood.[31]

30. John Crook, 'The Yogins of Ladakh' in Crook and Osmaston, ed., *Himalayan Buddhist Villages,* 1986, p. 669.

31. Giuseppe Tucci, n. 16, p. 67.

The Kadampa school also believed in a similar mystical way and they followed the meditative techniques of illuminative analysis and a deliberative stilling of the mind called in Sanskrit respectively as Vipaśyana and Samatha. By employing these techniques, the discursive process that we call reason was silenced and a luminous motionless purity was set in form that was identified with a state of Buddhahood. Modern Western psychiatry has come closer to explaining such a state of mind as 'no mind' when the mind is free from the thinking process and is in a stage of tranquillity. In the Kagyupa and the Nyingmapa school the *Geshe* were divided into two categories like the Gelugpa's and in both these schools, the teaching took on two forms: the *shitra* based on scriptures and the *trup* based on mystical experiences with the highest title being called *Trupla* 'Master of Mystic Powers'.[32] The Nyingmapa's education system emphasised the role of retreats. After preliminary training in the Tibetan language and study of basic teachings, monks used to go to the mountains for meditational retreats. In the Dorje Drak monastery one of the bigger Nyingmapa monasteries, which had come up since eighteenth century, four monks used to go for tetreats every year to meditate on the preliminary practices of the *dzogchen* tradition. In both these traditions the mystic element was given a place of pride while among the reformed schools there was a process to sublimate their importance. Not much is known about the Bon system of education as to their gradation and awarding of degrees but from some scattered references we can glean that they also followed the reading of the Bon Kangyur and Tengyur and similar mystical procedures, though in Buddhist schools the practical procedures of Yogic techniques remained different. It could be said that the means are different but the end is the same. Like Buddhists, the Bonpos also followed the practice of debating in their monasteries.

The practice of debate was a very important part of the Tibetan education system whose roots can be traced back to Indian monasticism. In early Buddhism there were daily

32. Giuseppe Tucci, p. 84.

disputations between the Buddhists and the brāhmaṇas, which led to a system of community feeling and organ-isation among the Buddhists under the leadership of a learned and erudite monk. The *bhikkhus* also constantly kept on debating and clarifying with the Śākyamuni on points of discipline and practices which are mentioned in the *Vinaya Piṭaka.*[33] Doctrinal points occupied the centre stage of debate and it was precisely on matters of doctrine that difference among the sects arose. The Sanskrit word for debate is *vāda* which also conveys the meaning of a 'view' or a school of thought but is used mostly as a debate in the Buddhist context. In Tibet there took place a debate in Samye during the time of king Trisong Detsen in which a discussion went on between the Chinese, monk Hoshang and an Indian Kamalaśīla (monk) over which version of Buddhism should be introduced in Tibet and the matter was settled by debate which ultimately ended with the Indian point of view emerging triumphant.[34]

The final aim in monastic education was to gain transcending wisdom and compassion which was to be achieved by method of listening, examining and meditating, called *Thosamgomsum,* which would achieve the immediate purpose of *Khetsungzangsum* (erudition, self-control and kindness) as all the Buddhist practices were based on the trilogy of hearing, thinking and meditating on the doctrine. As ignorance was the root cause of all suffering and wisdom was the only way to extinguish this, so one needed to posit the correct view which even a learned man could at times not do because his analytical faculties become blurred due to a wrong understanding as the greatest achievements and limitation of the human mind is the constant acquisition of knowledge. Keeping this in mind, great importance was given to debate as a form of teaching right from the primary stage. The central purpose of debate was the practical application

---

33. *Vinaya Texts, The Cullavagga*, I.16,1.

34. *The Blue Annals*, p. 41, But Li-An-Che's view is that in such a form of debate the meditation school is bound to lose for the logic of the school does not indulge in verbal communication. Li-An-Che, *History of Tibetan Religion: A study in the Field,* 1994, p. 23.

of the doctrine, which are clouded by mis-conceptions and objections to the correct view and more positively to establish the correct view. Thus, valid cognition as a subject was studied intermittently throughout the course.

For the monks, debate was just not another subject of mere academic study but was a way of using direct implications from the obvious in order to generate an inference of the non-obvious state of phenomena. The beginnings of debate in the educational career of a monk started from the time he was enrolled, and for whose benefit a senior lama explained the symbols behind the debate to get him acquainted with the technicalities during his first examination, he was asked to recite by heart from the texts and was questioned but this was not debate *per se*. The young monk watched the debates and then learnt its rudiments, as he was not allowed to debate with the seniors even if he was a *getsul* or *gelong.*[35]

The case of the debating methodology consisted of learning a few solidly established basic forms of reasoning and its application to many different subjects.[36] At the out-set, the monks began with basic logic and some texts of India that consisted of both Sūtras and commentaries.

The advanced degree of *Geshe* was given only after the candidate proved his worth in debating skills. This was one of the high points of his career when his analytical faculties were so developed as to subtly reason and employ discriminatory skills, which in turn helped in appreciation of scriptures. Such a person could now apply as many as twenty logical arguments to just one point of teaching.

According to the Buddhist cosmology, all phenomena in the universe are impermanent, therefore anything functional is impermanent, because of its being instantaneous since it was created by some causes and when the causes themselves are no longer present the phenomena disappear. This was

35. L.A. Wadell, n. 12, pp. 170-79.

36. Tsung Lien Shen and Shen Chien Liu, *The Tibetans,* 1953, p. 81.

the Buddhist theory of cause and effect, and being one of the fundamental principles of Buddhist theory acquiring proficiency in this topic was a must. For only when the message reaches the people can it be deemed to have been practically applied, as the fourteenth Dalai Lama says that it was best if one can have both learnedness and a sense of practical application. But having to choose, then a 'sense of practical application would be more important'.[37]

The debates were held in the courtyards of the monasteries and were a daily affair with individual monks debating with each other. But public debates were held in certain gardens and places set apart for this specific purpose in the monastery called *chottra,* which literally meant *dharma* schools. In such formal debates there was usually an abbot or a notable with the topic being a point of doctrinal inter-pretation of a text or its meaning. Hence, it was well attended as it helped to satisfy the doubts of the other monks and for the laity, the theatrical way in which the whole debate proceeded attracted them. The defender sat in front of the challenger who stood before him and shot rapid fire questions, while assuming threatening postures which, while lending an atmosphere of theatrics, would lead a first timer to conclude that the monks were on the verge of violence. The aggressive postures they assumed had significance and can be explained semiotically while the whole action could said to be bordering an art form. This was obviously a remnant of the great martial tradition of the Tibetans. The challenger's questions were answered with syllogisms, example and quotations in a quick pace. But the only drawback of such a momentous and innovative aid in the system of knowledge was the staidness and lack of originality of the debators. That indicated the state of affairs that things had come to a pass and the specific purpose for which rituals were designed had become formalities. Though it was not the case with all debators, as some did show originality.

The early Buddhist *saṁgha* was not organised as a

---

37. Daniel Perdue, *Debate in Tibetan Buddhist Education*, 1976, p. 7.

spiritual hierarchy but rather as an association of individuals seeking salvation for themselves and also for others. European scholars see Lamaism as a religious hierarchy and thus the term 'Lamaist hierarchy' is used frequently.[38] At the core of this argument regarding Tibet, is that one has to draw a line of demarcation between the role of monks in the monastery and in the society as they served in both spiritual and temporal capacities. As a member of the monastery he was subject to its rules and was assigned powers in relation to position, while on the other hand, as an official he was on par with the lay officials and all his deeds were accountable in the administrative capacity. The early Buddhist *saṁgha* needed the monks to serve in a variety of capacities for the smooth functioning and allocation of day-to-day activities but two points need to be stressed here regarding the role of officials in the monastery. First, the abbot's office was by election and secondly, monks owed no obedience, in the sense that any fetters did not bind them.

But in Tibet among the Nyingmapas and the Śākyapas abbotship passed from the father to the son and from uncle to nephew respectively. As we have seen that the head of the monk was either an incarnate lama called *trulku* or *kusso,* both of whon were appointed because of the special circumstance surrounding their birth. In other cases where the posts were not reserved for the reincarnate lamas, the Khenpo was the head of the monastery and was chosen by election. Thus, at the apex of the monastic organisation was the Khenpo or Kusso whose post in English can be translated as abbot. The term lama was, strictly speaking, used only for *trulku*s (incarnate lamas) and *guru*s who give formal discourses regardless of their being *Geshe*s or *gelong*s. Therefore, the term lama was not the synonym for a monk. The abbot or *khenpo* had a fixed term for three years after which he becomes an abbot emeritus. Abbots were chosen from among the assistant abbots (*Lama-u-dza*) which was also a part of the reforms of the thirteenth Dalai Lama and

38. Tsung Lien Shen, n. 36, pp. 84-6, also see L.A. Waddell, n. 12, pp. 234-57.

the qualifications were that only *Geshe Lha-rampas* could become assistant abbots of monasteries and so logically only they could advance to the higher posts automatically after a three year term. After becoming the abbot of a Tāntric monastery, he must retire and become an abbot emeritus (*Kanzur rinpoche*). This was his final stage after which two options were open to him, either continue teaching as a great *guru* which was of a highly exalted nature as he commanded reverence on account of his teaching or go into the mountains or a secluded spot for further studies or do a formal Tāntric retreat. The most obvious outcome of such an arrangement, in terms of monastic power-play was to eliminate the abbot from competing for the post again and again, reducing its prestige thereby, and removing potentialities for groupism and lobbying.

As we have seen earlier the three main components of a monastery were the La-chi (university board), Dra-Tsang (college) and Khamtsen (dormitory). In smaller monasteries there was only one Khenpo but in larger monasteries each Dra-Tsang was held by a Khenpo who had the overall charge of all the internal affairs of the Dra-Tsang and who was also the representative of the Dra-Tsang in its dealings with other bodies like the Khamtsen and more with the La-chi. The main functions of the Khenpo included overseeing the disciplinary proceedings apart form the day-to-day activities of Dra-tsang. For this, he was assisted by a committee, the most important members of which were the steward, spyi-nyer who was incharge of general affairs including finance, the choir leader and the proctor.

The unit which came under the Dra-tsang was the Khamtsen, organised on a similar pattern like the Dra-tsang as both were financially self-contained units with a difference that the Khamtsen had no financial commitments to the Dra-tsang though it had share in the revenues of the Dra-tsang. Unlike the Dra-tsang, the Khamtsen had regional identity with new adherents joining the Khamtsen of the region or the linguistic area they hailed from, with many of them even having kinship connections. In the Drepung monastery there were separate Khamtsens for students coming from as far as Mongolia, Kalmyk regions, etc., and judging by the size of a Khamtsen, again in the Drepung monastery the largest Dra-tsang had twenty-three Khamtsens under it. The affairs of the Khamtsen were not run by Khenpos but by a committee headed by a senior which was filled up by rotation, with every senior having to compulsorily serve under the senior who headed the committee. The post was ornamental and was no big attraction that was just the reason for seniors being made to serve compulsorily. As the service here has more of work and responsibility than reward it was viewed as a sort of burden which the financially sound candidates seeked to bypass by paying a stipulated amount of exemption fee. This was also a pointer to some elitist bias in the monastic organisation. The overall discipline and curriculum of the Khamtsen were subject to control by the Dra-tsang.

The La-chi that was the university board has a committee composed of all the Khenpos who were the presidents of the respective Dra-tsangs along with other Dra-tsang committee members who were posted in this La-chi commitee but under titles different from what they held in their respective Dra-tsang.

The Khenpo or the Kusso who functioned as the abbot, with an assistant abbot under him as we have seen headed the typical administrative organisation in a *gompa*. The day-to-day activities necessitated a hierarchy of officials with specifically assigned duties akin to a bureaucratic enterprise which were as follows.

1. Lob-pon, i.e., the professor or ordained monk who proclaimed the law and regulated conduct.
2. C'ag-dso was the treasurer or cashier.
3. Ner-pa or spyi-ner was the steward who managed the day-to-day requirements of the institution. Both these posts involved a lot of work as the *gompa* was involved in a multitude of economic transactions and also a big consumer of produce.

4. Ge-ko was incharge of law and order, leading us to wonder whether the whole organisation was not self-regulatory. In fact, the Ge-ko was harsh in the application of law not hesitating to use the cane, a frequent punishment for minor infringements.
5. The orderlies who assisted him in such exercises were called Hag-ner.
6. Um-dse was the officer of ceremonies.
7. Ku-ner was the sacristan responsible for the care of holy books and other movable property of the *gompa.*
8. Ja-ma served tea, the national beverage and food to the monks.
9. Ch'ab-dren served water.
10. Spyi-k'yab was the secretary.
11. Gsal-dpon was the cook.
12. Gzim-dpon was the chamberlain
13. Mgron-gna-ch'en was the warden incharge of hospitality.
14. Tsi-dpon was the keeper of accounts.
15. P'yag-tsang was the bearer of the monastic emblem.[39]

The above list is not exhaustive as many *gompa*s performed other functions thereby accommodating monks in diverse capacities. An example was the famous Narthang monastery in eastern Tibet, which was a well-known centre for printing where the majority of monks could be called 'artisans'. There was also an impression conveyed by earlier writers who fail to mention the large body of illiterate monks thereby giving the impression that the *gompa* was filled with only erudite monks engaged in religious speculation. Scholars like Sir Charles Bell, Kawaguchi, etc., have pointed out to

---

39. O.C. Handa, n 22, p. 137.

the existence of a large body of illiterate monks whom they encountered in the course of their journeys. The Tibetan name for the lama warriors (Do Tho) means villains. Their origin is a matter of historical enquiry not yet settled due to paucity of references in works such as the *Blue Annals* whose main preoccupation seem to be dates and personalities. The lama warriors in all probability came up during the thirteenth-fourteenth centuries when Tibet was engulfed in intense sectarian rivalry and monasteries became power centres. So these lamas may have been the residue of the warrior element whose function was to protect the *gompa*s against attacks, later substituted to guarding the monastery premises, accompany trade caravans and serve as bodyguards of high lamas when travelling. They maintained strict secrecy about their cult and in dress and gait, in contrast to the simple demure lamas by growing long hair curled in plaits, their aprons bearing weapons at times. Gymnastics and other physical exercises were performed by them which they put to good use during the regulation of the festival, Great Prayer Festival (*Monlam Chenmo*) the whole administration of Lhasa passed down to the warrior monks of Drepung for ten days.[40]

It would be out of place if *ani-gompa*s are not mentioned. Women functioned as religious practitioners in pre-modern Tibet in a variety of capacities as *cha-kha*(s) and *dpamo*(s) (spirit mediums), female religious bards called *ma-ni-pa*(s) and nuns were called *ani*(s). That is they functioned at all levels of the Buddhist religious activity from Tāntric adepts to nuns. According to some figures, around two per cent of the population were nuns which was only a shadow compared to that of monks but nevertheless very important as it shows that women were not excluded because of their sex. Among the famous *ani-gompa*s mention may be made of Samding *gompa*[41] which was the state nunnery of Tibet and its abbess was regarded as the incarnation of the deity rDo-rje Phags-mo

40. Charles Bell, *The Religion of Tibet*, 1992, p. 169.
41. Janice D. Willis, 'Tibetan Ani-s; The Nun's life in Tibet', *The Tibet Journal*, vol. 9, no. 4, Winter 1984, p. 15.

(Skt. Vajravārāhī). *Ani-gompa*s did not scale the heights of the regular *gompa*s but their contribution cannot he denied.

Conclusion

The rudimentary beginnings of a settled monastic life can be traced from the time of Lord Buddha when the monastic code was developing. Side by side a high premium was placed on education which became the major pre-occupation as the *vihāra* was well endowed by patrons. The post-Gupta period saw the beginnings of the *mahāvihāra*s and by the Pāla times, Tibetan presence in the *mahāvihāra*s of Vikramaśilā, Oḍantapurī and Nālandā was almost two centureis old. Such monasteries provided the models for Tibetan monasteries which sprang up in profusion in the post Langdarma period. Education, along with the conduct of rituals, the latter being given a high place in Mahāyāna Buddhism were the major pre-occupations of the newly established Tibetan *gompa*s. Patronage led to the founding of newer and bigger monasteries, the high point of which was the establishment of Sera, Ganden and Drepung, which could be called monastic towns.

Education was organised on a standard pattern with each sect stressing their own teachings. Reforms in monastic education by the fifth Dalai Lama saw the *Geshe* degree originally instituted by the Sakyapas being streamlined. Medicine, astronomy, painting, etc., also figured as subjects of study in the monastery. The management of all these affairs necessitated an organisational network leading to the *gompa* being organised on a hierarchical basis with the Khenpo at the top, who looked over the different officials who had specific duties like enforcing discipline, managing, accounts, etc. All monks were not involved in education and there also existed a class of warrior monks. In the *gompa*s, the residential units, that is the Dra-tsangs, were managed and maintained wholly by the community with which it was deeply involved. It may thus be said that the monastery was a part of the society, yet detached from it.

4

Gompa and Art and Architecture

TIBETAN art and literature are overwhelmingly religious, that at a first glance, it leads us to conclude that there was no other secular art form. But the reality is that among the remains of Tibet art and architecture though everything has religious association, as religion was a living tradition with art and architecture being very integral parts of it. Secular art is found, but in ruins and in a bad state of preservation, with specimens also very rare, amounting to just a handful. The *gompa*s that were found in all possible locations ranging from open fields, trade routes to inaccessible and strategic locations are the main repositories of Tibetan art. Artefacts within the *gompa* were the paintings called *thanka*s (oncloth) which were found in profusion. Appliqué banners, mural paintings, statues, religious artefacts like the *dorje* (thunderbolt), *dribul* (bell) were essential accompaniments. No space was spared and we have expressions of art on rocks, *maṇi*-walls, *kaṅkaṇī*s, *toraṇa*s, butter sculpture and prayer wheels that complete the assortment of Tibetan art in addition to icons of metal and some in stone.

Changes in Tibetan art and architecture can be seen with coeval changes in society, culture and patronage, that over the centuries led to changes stylistically and technically. At some junctures it is nearly impossible to find the source of the influence. Indian influences are as important and have exerted a considerable attention but it would be unjust not to acknowledge other influences particularly Nepalese,[1] Chinese and to an extent Xixia,[2] etc.

Monastic architecture

Painting and the plastic arts offer greater scope for creativity and, hence, mirrored changes in religion and society more dynamically rather than architecture. The architectural examples are the *gompa*s and the *Chortens* (Tib. *mchodrten* Skt. *stūpa*) which offered less room for creativity, restrained due to terrain and building materials. Two periods of development can be traced with regard to *gompa*s, the first is the early period up to the fourteenth century AD, while the later period started from the fourteenth century and extended up to the modern period.

A survey of the development of the early monasteries in India would help us to put in clear light the changes in later stages and the Tibetan contributions to the building tradition. We had already seen that the three wet months during the rainy season led to the practice of *Vassavassa,* which was a period of introspection and rest. These settlements were called the *avasa*s and *arama*s, originally semi-permanent settlements becoming permanent even during the life of the Master. Lord Buddha had even answered to the queries of the *bhikkhu*s regarding their stay and construction of monasteries. Settlements in the forest areas were far and few, the majority of the settlements being in rural and urban areas, the *avasa*s and *arama*s were respectively endowed by the patrons. Monasticism attracted many adherents leading to their proliferation all over eastern and northern India. During this expansion of the monastery premises, there emerged the *lena.* Needs of the monks were now manifold like space for residence, training of novices and other functions like ceremonies and collective rituals for which the earlier *avasa* and *arama,* both of which were simpler could

1. Krishna Ghosh, *Few Tibetan Deities,* Ph.D. Thesis, 1996, p. 96, see also Charles Bell, *People of Tibet,* 1991, rpt., p. 119 talks of Newars in Lhasa, Shigatse and Gyantse.
2. R.A. Stein, *Tibetan Civilization,* J.E. Stapleton Driver, tr., 1972, p. 283.

not fully suffice. Thus, developed the Buddhist monastery from the simple *vassavassa* to the *saṁghārāma* and *avasa* to a *lena* reflecting stages in the complexities of organisation and rituals. The *lena* was a settled body of monks functionally a *saṁgha* by itself. The *Culavagga* defines five kinds of *lena* which are fit as dwelling places for monks as *vihāra, addhayoga, pāsāda, hammīya* and *guha*.[3] Functionally the increased number of inmates and the patronage of the rich had direct bearings like the increased need for kitchens to feed the monkhood, *upathamaśālā* or common meeting hall for the *uposatha* and *pātimokkha* ceremonies and other collective rituals, stores for the grains and other possession which were mainly donations, wells which served as a source of water.[4] Patronage also had its effect on the style with brick coming into vogue as a replacement for wood, finally leading to solid structures made of stone and brick.

The fourth century AD, the period of the Guptas saw the *vihāra*s being transformed into *mahāvihāra*s (monastic universities) which were grandiose buildings built of brick[5] and stone. Nālandā, Vikramaśilā, Oḍantapurī and Dhanyakaṭaka, just to name a few were the notable *mahāvihāra*s whose fame spręad beyond borders. These monasteries are very important for the study of Tibetan history as the Tibetan *gompa*s were built on their prototypes. The Indian *mahāvihāra*s were multi-storeyed buildings built of stone and on flat ground whereas the situation in Tibet was quite different. Firstly Tibet was a mountainous country with valleys and secondly there is scarcity of both good quality stone and also of wood which were used in abundance in Indian monasteries.

Samye, the earliest monastery of Tibet was built on the model of the Oḍantapurī monastery of eastern India in AD 749, after which came up other famous monasteries of Tibet

3. *Vinaya Texts, The Cullavagga*, Vl.1, 2.
4. *Ibid.*, VI.3, 6.
5. Sukumar Dutt, *Buddhist Monks and Monasteries of India*, 1962, p. 200.

such as Ramoche in Lhasa built on the model of the Vikramaśilā monastery of Bengal during the time of Padmasambhava.[6] Some authors speculate on Chinese influence in Ramoche and by extension on the early architecture of Tibet based on Ramoche as it has the famous Jowo-Khang temple,[7] one of the most sacred and earliest of Tibet's scared spots which enshrined the image of Buddha brought by Wen Cheng the wife of Songsten Gampo. Incidentally there is also an image of Akṣobhaya Buddha brought here by the Nepalese wife of Songtsen Gampo, Bhr̥kuṭi Devī. Tholing monastery in the western Tibetan Kingdom of Guge which spearheaded the Buddhist revival during the post Lang-darma period saw hectic construction activity during the time of the famous Lotsba Rinchen Zangpo and his able patron Yeshe 'Ö' to whom a hundred and eight monas-teries are credited, chief of which is Tholing built aroud AD 1000 modelled on the Vikramaśilā monastery. Other famous Tibetan monasteries of the early period that were modelled on Indian prototypes were the Guru Cho'Wan monastery near Bhutan built during the time of Padmasambhava modelled on the famous Nālandā *mahāvihāra.* Chronologically the last to be built, Drepung was the largest, most powerful and populous of all the monasteries of Tibet was built on the prototype of the great monastery of Dhanyakaṭaka in south India.[8] All these monasteries were built till the thirteenth century, and precisely speaking between the eleventh and the thirteenth centuries when the building activity was at its peak.

The monasteries of the early period had many similarities in terms of layout, plan and construction techniques with their Indian prototypes. However, certain features needed to be modified to suit the terrain and raw materials. Other factors included the tradition that deemed some signs as good omens, all of which led to a new language in construction of monasteries. There existed in India a treatise called the *Saddharmasmr̥tyupasthāna Sūtra* that provided the

6. Victor Chan, *Tibet Handbook,* 1994, pp. 116-18.
7. *Ibid.*
8. *Ibid.,* p. 145.

guidelines for temple construction. The Indian style blended with native genius and was called the *rgya-gar-gyi-khang,* which means the Indian style of architecture.

Early monasteries that sprang up in Tibet were to an extent influenced by Nepal as elements of the then Buddhist culture of Pāla eastern India reached Tibet through Nepal. Evidences of this are the Nepalese type of treatment of *hārmika* in the *stūpa* which reached Tibet.[9] Trade routes between Tibet and Nepal were rather secure, free of brigandage prompting Padmasambhava to visit Tibet via Nepal. Like central Tibet, western Tibet in the early phases of monastic activity, i.e., pre-Langdarma period did not have many monasteries to speak of. The western Tibetan Buddhist revival which saw monastery building on a large-scale under the able watch of Rinchen Zangpo had special features, a commonality was that the vast majority of the structures were single storeyed buildings devoid of grandeur, simple looking and spartan. They were all situated on flat ground like Tabo, Alchi, Kanum, etc., which gave them ample scope to expand vertically rather than horizontally.[10]

The Tibetans did not have to pass through the evolution of the Buddhist monastery over a long period of time (sixth century BC to seventh century AD), as in India. The Indian *mahāvihāra*s were the prototypes which found expression in the various *chos-khor*'s like Alchi, and Tabo. The *maṇḍala* concept of layout founds expression in this early structures according to which there was a centre, deemed to be sacred surrounding which there were concentric circles. In this case a central shrine surrounded by lesser important shrines at the outer periphery. Living rooms for the monks, libraries are also found in the outer periphery, the whole structure symbolising order and harmony. A boundary wall (Skt. *sīmā, Tib. Cags-ri*), encircled the whole complex and was a direct adaptation of the ancient Indian practice of marking off the

9. Robert E. Fisher, *Buddhist Art and Architecture,* 1993, pp. 72-85.
10. Romi Khosla, *Buddhist Monastries in the Western Himalayas,* 1979, p. 36.

sacred space from the other-worldly. Such practices have been found in the layout of early *avasas* and Indian temples.

Similar Indian practices of good omens contributed to the emergence of a Tibetan geomantic tradition, coupled with ritual, based on symbolism greatly determining the process of selection of a site, though practical considerations were never lost sight of. Thubten Legshay Gyatsho in his book *Gateway to the Temple* explains in great detail the complex processes that go into the selection of a site, begining with the first step in the construction of a *gompa*. Eight favourable attributes taken into consideration say the site should be located on a hill with land sloping away from the monastery and the site should contain a source of water and if there are any streams to the left or right of the monastery, or facing a body of water or waterfall were all considered ideal attributes.[11] The lama's and the architects then went on to test the soil by digging out a foot of the soil and then putting it back in the hole. If it covered the displaced place fully then the soil was good, if it sank too much leaving some space, then the soil could not bear the enormous load. It was quite a tough search to get all the attributes mentioned in the tradition. So necessary rituals were undertaken at the right time to ward off the evil spirits and placate the deities.

A strange feature observed in Tibet with regard to the *gompas* was the uniformity in style practised all over Tibet that was in sharp contrast to the domestic architecture where each region had a vernacular style. Only in Mongolia could we find the movable *gompas* made of tents. All *gompas* were oriented towards the south to catch the low winter sun of Tibet, and in this respect of orientation the monastic and domestic architecture were agreed upon. Western Tibetan nomadic tents, monasteries of Ladakh to a great extent and all of Sikkim, Bhutan and Himachal Pradesh are oriented towards the east to catch the early rays of the rising sun.[12]

---

11. Thubeten Legshay Gyatsho, *Gateway to the Temple*, 1979, pp. 29-30.
12. William Semple, 'Symbolism and Ritual in Tibetan Architecture', *Choyang*, vol. 3, 1993, p. 141.

Leaving aside these minor variations, *gompas* all over Tibet exhibited striking similarities in construction techniques layout and planning with the only constraint being resources which were scarce in the remote agricultural communities leading to smaller *gompas* there. Symbolism was very much a part of the Tibetan psyche as every object has a meaning expressed even in the orientation of the monasteries were the five elements symbolising the directions, again part of a great *maṇḍala*.

Tibet and the whole of Central Asia share the same geoclimatic features, characterised by shortage of vegetation the only vegetation, found are grass and shrubs with few trees. Good quality stones were also hard to come by therefore leaving scope only for clay that is the prime building material. The arid climate coupled with the absence of rainfall made mud a good alternative to stone and wood. Being plastic material mud was a favoured medium for building but the possibilities were limited on account of the shapes into which it could take forms, particularly restricted to blocks. The first step was that the mud was made into nice dough akin to wheat being made as a batter. The whole batter was then checked for consistency to render into it toughness wherein lied the secret of the durability. The semi-solid mixture was skillfully cast into moulds that are then removed carefully after adequate compression so as to eliminate air bubbles and prevent cracking at the edges, which would reduce the durability. Sun-dried bricks were then ready for use. During times of water scarcity it was prohibited to undertake any building activity, as it would tell on the scarce water resources.[13]

After the foundation had been laid in accordance with the rituals, the building activity proper commenced. Vernacular and monastic architecture were both similar when finished as they were both box-life structures due to the limited possibilities of design that brick offers. Storey upon storey was built with bricks, the lowest storey having the

13. Charles Bell, n. 1, p. 39.

thickest walls to take the load of the massive structure, gradually tapering towards the top. Even in such an activity as building a wall which is a plane structure, the Tibetan notion of symbolism had entered with the bricks arranged in a layer of thick and thin alternatively, symbolising the union of the male and the female, a cardinal theme of Tāntric Buddhism.[14]

In the interiors were the massive wooden columns and beams to support the great load of the successive floors and roof, all made of brick in a box type fashion. In the *gompas* of the early period the columns were placed in the form of a *maṇḍala*. Alchi is a typical example of such arrangement and it has a lot of Kāśmīrī influence in the woodwork and stone.[15] Openings were very few in the lower floors to protect against the biting cold and they increased as they go up. The lowest floor was reserved for animals while the abbot or Khenpo occupied the highest room symbolic of his superordinate status. This in brief is a description of the architectural features of the *gompa* from its inception in the seventh till the thirteenth centuries.

The later decades of the thirteenth and the fourteenth centuries saw large-scale political and social turmoil in both India and Tibet which had far-reaching consequences for monasticism. The Turkish conquest of northern and eastern India led to the destruction of Buddhist monasteries and by extension Buddhism itself, as the monastery was the organised head of the faith. Centuries long association with Tibet came to an end and the links were severed once and for all. In Tibet itself the rise of the Mongols in polity and their consequent support to the Sakyapas changed the character of Buddhism from a purely spiritual religion to that of a religion involved in temporal affairs. This is not to contest the fact that the *gompas* of the early period were not oriented to politics. They surely were, but in an indirect way as

---

14. William Semple, n. 12, p. 114.

15. David Snellgrove and Taduesz Skopurski, *The Cutural Heritage of Ladakh,* vol. 1, 1977, pp. 23-8.

outposts of the political structure in the outlying areas never to have any direct dealing in the temporal process. During this preiod, i.e., thirteenth to fourteenth century AD, Indian style was partly replaced by *rgya-nag* or Chinese style as China was also part of the Mongol Empire leading to greater cultural intercourse with China. Indian elements were neither fully eliminated nor did Chinese elements predominate but the militaristic elements set the agenda for the architectural development.

Sectarian feuds engulfed the Tibetan landscape prompting the monasteries to be built on hillocks that were at a vantage point to ward of the intruders, also facilitating a command over the entire valley below, in such a condition the *maṇḍala* system of layout could not be adhered to. The box type structures comprising the various rooms were arranged on the hillock in a haphazard manner giving a look of pyramidal mass and solidity. Lack of space and the need to follow the natural contours of the hill led to the temples being jammed in the midst of the functional apartments. The latter are seen in profusion as a reflection of the needs of the times, which dictated the need for more and more space for administrative establishments. The Dzongs of Bhutan are the classical example of such a synthesis of military, bureaucratic and religious set-up in an institution. Such compulsions dictated the ancient monastery of Rangrik to be relocated and rebuilt on top of a hillock at Ki.[16]

Sera, Ganden and Drepung, the famous triumvirate of the Tibetan monastic set-up along with Tasilhunpo in Central Tibet, Punakha Dzong and Paro Dzong in Bhutan, Ki, Tangyud and Dhankar in the Spiti valley, Hemis, Phyang, Likir, Rangdum in Ladakh to name a few, were built on the pattern of later monasteries imbibing a fortress like quality.[17] The main features of such are the specialised functions of residential quarters, the military and religious requirements.

16. O.C. Handa, *Buddhist Monasteries in Himachal Pradesh,* 1987, p. 148.
17. Romi Khosla, n. 10, p. 78.

Multistoreyed buildings became common as the Tibetans were now fully used to running large monasteries. Moreover the needs of the community and their dependence on the monasteries had also increased. The style that came to predominate is called the Central Tibetan style. The entrance to these monasteries was made through the courtyard, the only available open space as no space could be spared on the hill top. Courtyards played a vital role in the life of the community as congregation centres during times of the annual festivals when the *Cham* dances took place. Crossing the courtyard, one then entered the entrance portico which led to the *du-khang* (assembly room) and the entrance portico here, is symbolically conceived of as a link to the sacred world, in line with the *maṇḍala* theory of the ancient Indian system of architecture.

Around the sacred temple, the *lha-khang* (god's room) were prayer wheels inscribed with the sacred words *OṀ MAṆI PADME HUṀ* which the pilgrim kept on rotating as he circumambulated the passage once, twice or a hundred and eight times. Finally he reached the *du-khang* and the *lha-khang*, the two most important and sacred rooms built in a square or rectangular fashion. The images and altars were placed against the end wall enabling rows of monks to sit in rooms facing each other across the central aisle. Other important rooms were the *zimchung,* the personal room of the head lama usually located in a position that had a clear view of the courtyard, and included within the main temple complex or was a separate cloister, in any case situated at a commanding height having its own altar, a bed and a toilet. The *gon khang* is also called by many writers as the chamber of horrors, housing the fearsome images of Tāntric divinities.

Finally we come to the Dra-tsang's or cells of the monks for which the monastery was not responsible and the building plus the upkeep of it was the responsibility of the monks or their families.[18] Stores were there for cooking in the kitchen near which were situated the storerooms. Monks performed

---

18. Tsung Lien Shen and Shen Chien Liu, *The Tibetans,* 1953, p. 73.

their ablutions in the toilets attached to the cells directly connected to chutes leading the waste material down. It was a good source of manure for the villagers who collect it after certain period of time, and constant washing of the toilet helped to keep it free from smell.

Surrounding the monasteries were the *chorten*s (Skt. *stūpa*) a reliquary and votive object originally intended to hold the relics of the Buddha after his *mahāparinirvāṇa.*[19] Sāñcī *stūpa is* the most famous and typical example of a *stūpa* that contains a bulbous dome called the *aṇḍa*, on top of which is a finial called the *hārmika,* the whole enclosure was surrounded by a railing and was used as a circum-ambulatory passage. Entrance was through a gateway called the *toraṇa,* an object of ornamentation that is at a considerable remove from the simplistic practices of early Buddhism. In addition to the above-mentioned three functions, the *chorten*s in Tibet enshrined the relics of high lamas or votive objects like clay tablets called *tsa-tsa.*[20] Being imbued with symbolism the *chorten* become an object of concentration, hence it was commissioned to be made out of clay and metal in miniature.

Caitya-vibhaṅga Vinayoddhṛta-Sūtra is the last Sanskrit original manuscript available in Tibetan called *Mchodrton gyi cha dbye ba'dul ba las byung ba'vinda* which explains in detail the symbolic meaning of the *chorten.*[21] Exoterically, the five different parts of the *chorten* represent the five primal elements with the square core representing the Earth, the stylised dome representing water, the tapering shaft representing fire, the crescent representing the element of air and the acuminated circle at the top representing the element of ether. According to rigid architectural canons, the body of the Buddha was taken to be the perfect body and divided into nine spans for iconometric purposes called the *nava-tāla*

19. Adrian Snodgrass, *The Symbolism of the Stupa,* 1992, p. 353.
20. Giuseppe Tucci, *Tibet: Land of Snows,* J.E. Stapleton Driver, tr., 1967, p. 116.
21. Pema Dorjee, *Stupa and its Technology — A Tibeto-Buddhist Perspective,* 1996, p. 10.

system. The five elements should be proportionally divided according to the rules prescribed in the texts so as to symbolise the perfect human body. *Chortens* were of eight types as depicted in the *Kanisadisavyakama* (Tib *Liyul Lung Custan Pa*) of the *Tangyur* testament which outlines in detail the meaning of the eight types of *chortens* which symbolise the eight great events in the life of the Buddha sequentially in order, they are as follows:

1. *Kutam chorten* symbolises the nativity of Buddha.
2. *Labab chorten* symbolises the celestial visit of Buddha and his return to earth, the ladder symbolises this event.
3. *Namgyal chorten* symbolises the life giving powers of *uṣṇīṣavijaya*.
4. *Chotul chorten* symbolises the Buddha's spiritual powers.
5. *Dutul chorten* commemorates the Buddha's victory over evil.
6. *Jangshub chorten* symbolises Buddha's final enlightenment.
7. *Papung chorten* represents the Buddha teaching on the three vehicles.
8. *Myangda chortern* commemorates the Buddha's attainment of the highest *nirvāṇa*.

Massivity in size came to be viewed as a positive earner of merit proportionately and the *chortens* also came to be built of very massive size, the best example of which is the *chorten* at Gyantse, which was also a celebration of power. A gigantic multistoreyed structure betraying Nepalese influence seen in the painted eyes at the top, this *chorten* could be entered inside with staircases allowing the pilgrims to go upwards and pay obeisance to the deities.[22] Scarce

22. Thubten Legshay Gyatsho, n. 11, pp. 62-6.

openings created abundant space on the interior of the walls, providing a canvas for the larger than life size murals. Tibetan *chortens* had a uniformity all over the Tibetan culture area without any stylistic variations, strictly adhering to the rigid canons expounded in the text and as a practice from the first quarter of the fourteenth century, the period of Gelugpa rule.[23] Stylistically both the *gompa* and the *chorten* remained unchanged over the centuries reflecting the deep conservatism among the people.

The subject-matter of Tibetan art and their treatment

Tibetan art is portrayed as a complex pantheon of terrifying deities in aggressive postures and strong colours along with sexual imagery. The truth is that a vast majority of the Tibetan pantheon originated from India where the abovesaid deities were part of the Tāntric Buddhism. To the second part, Tāntric had been assigned a place as degenerate Buddhism (a very derogatory and objectionable term used by earlier historians) given in to licentiousness, examples of which are the *yab-yum* statues. But the truth cannot be farther from this for *tantra* is not understood as a conceptual system but as degenerate Buddhism.

The overwhelming majority of the paintings and sculptures had the Buddha in his various manifestations as their subjects. The deities can be divided into serene and wrathful. To the first category belong the Buddhas, *bodhisattavas* and the Tārās along with the great Indian and Tibetan Masters. Their main features were slender figure, light colours, and particularly blue, white and green, rigidity in the postures in strict accordance with the iconographic canons.[24] The wrathful deities on the other hand are the *yidams* or tutelary deities, the guardian deities, Mahākāla, etc. They are depicted in aggressive postures, with elongated body parts like fat

---

23. Thubten Legshay Gyatsho, n. 11, pp. 70-1.
24. *Ibid.*, pp. 62-6.
25. *Ibid.*, pp. 70-1.

forearms, swollen bellies and big teeth.[25] The proportion is not rigid and the colours used are dark like blue, red and black with contrasts alternating very quickly while in the case of the serene deities the colours alternate in slow succession. During the first phase, best exemplified at Alchi, Tholing, etc., Indian influences predominated in painting with the Buddha depicted in Gāndhāra style, leaving vast spaces open in the background, less use of blue colour. The first phase is dated from seventh century AD. When Tibetan paintings are noticed till the fourteenth century AD. The trends noticed during the seventh-eleventh centuries are patronage extended to Buddhism by aristocratic and royal patrons. Kāśmīrī stylistic tradition is evident as the *Blue Annals* records many Tibetan monks going to Kāśmīr for study. Moreover, Kāśmīrī artists were famous and Rinchen Zangpo is said to have brought fifty-four Kāśmīrī artists to western Tibetan areas.[26] By AD 1200 the western Tibetan kingdom began to decline and the paintings at Alchi dated around AD 1200 are the last examples of this golden age. The focus then shifts to central Tibet under the patronage of the Sakyapas and the Kagyupas in the thirteenth and fourteenth centuries AD.[27] Central Asian and Chinese influences are evident in the treatment of paintings by including water falls, sceneries and paraphernalia in the vacant spaces. A concurrent development was the portrayal of the sectarian hirearchs particularly the Sakyapa's. Their charismatic appeal and spiritual achievements, all lavishly done immortalised the hirearchs. Features of personages are also sinicised with mongoloid[28] features replacing Earlier Gāndhāra features found in the western Tibetan area (e.g., Alchi, Tholing, Purang, etc).

Since the Mahāyānists believed in the transcendental nature (*lokottara*) of the Buddha, it gave rise to the portrayal of the Buddha as the *bodhisattva* in many forms, most

26. *The Blue Annals,* pp. 68, 72.
27. Pratapaditya Pal, *Tibetan Paintings,* 1998, p. 62.
28. Nirmal C. Sinha, *Tales the Thankas Tell — An Introduction to Tibetan Scroll Portaits,* 1989, p. 14.

popular and numerous of which predominated throughout the ages were the five Buddhas, i.e., the Dhyānī and Mortal Buddhas. The contemplative Buddhas could not be seen by the human beings and they live in Sukhāvatī (a paradise). Mortal Buddhas appeared on their behalf but the physical features of both were the same and paintings and sculptures depict the mood, colour gesture and symbol to identify them. Thus, while mentioning the five contemplative Buddhas, five corresponding Buddha's have been identified. They are as follows:

1. Amitābha corresponding to Avalokiteśvara (*bodhisattva*) with colour red.
2. Akṣobhaya is the second Buddha corresponding to Vajrapāṇi, with colour blue.
3. Vairocana corresponding to Krakuchanda with colour white.
4. Amogasiddhi corresponding to Viśvapāṇi with colour green.
5. Ratanasambhva corresponding to Kāśyapa with colour yellow.[29]

The above-mentioned five Buddhas, Green Tārā and white Tārā were the most prolific painted figures. *Yidams* or tutelary deities and *maṇḍala*s served the purpose of meditation for the adept, who during the course of meditation identified and modelled his personality in the course of practice recreating for him the sacred world of the deity.[30] The protector deities were the Tse-Rin-Mched-Lna (The five sisters of long life) and the Bstan-Ma-Bar Gns is (The twelve guardian goddesses)[31] who existed from pre-Buddhist times and their worship takes the roots of Tibetan subject-matter

---

29. Ven Melpittiye Wimalakitti, *A Comparative Analysis of Symbolism in Theravada and Mahayana Iconography,* Ph. D. Thesis, 1996, pp. 52-6.

30 David L. Snellgrove, n. 15, p. 14.

31. Krishna Ghosh, n. 1, p. 158.

to pre-Buddhist period. It is a well-known fact that Padmasambhava was challenged by these deities and his genius led to their defeat and incorporation into the Buddhist pantheon, a myth which has striking parallels to India wherein new deities were incorporated in tune with the Purāṇic ideology. Mahākāla (*mgon po*), a protector deity popular among the nomads has a countless retinue endowed with wisdom is one of the most often portrayed *yidams*. Black in colour with weaponry, protruding tongue, a chain of skulls on his neck, elongated arms, swollen stomach are his characteristics is actually an import from India. The popularity of these deities was that they served various purposes, which were of a spiritual nature.

Paintings depicting the mystical land of Shambala and its warriors symbolised the celebration of the martial spirit of the ancient Tibetans.[32] Art itself became a matter of contestation when the Gelugpas tried to rewrite the history by laying less stress on the earlier achievements of the princes of Gyantse who fostered the cult of the Dharmarājas and likened themselves to the Great Buddhist kings of Ancient Tibet. According to Erberto. F. Lo Brue in the main temple of the sacred enclave at Gyantse, the placing of the huge Maitreya statue in the middle of the *chos- rgyal-lha-khang* was probably meant to distort the iconographic programme which has been known by the name of *Byams-pai Lha-khang* (temple of Maitreya).[33]

The *maṇḍala* is another subject, which finds frequent mention, is a conceptually complex item used for religious purposes represents a cosmos in miniature. Apart from functioning as an aid in meditation, they were also commissioned in typical Buddhist fashion as a prayer for the welfare of the others.[34]

Buddhist concepts like the wheel of life were pictorially

32. Nirrnal C. Sinha, n. 26, pp. 15-16.

33. Erberto F. LO Brue, 'The Sacred Enclave of Gyantse' in Pratapaditya Pal, ed., *MARG,* vol. XLVIII, no. 1, pp. 45-50.

34. Robert E. Fisher, n. 9, p. 82.

expressed in the *thankas*. Here the wheel is life (*saṁsāra*) held in the grip of a demon symbolising *karma*. In the centre are a cock, snake and pig symbolising the three poisons of passion, hatred and delusion. They are surrounded by a circle divided into two halves, black and white, the former signifying people who do bad and the latter the people who do good and rise to higher realm while in the black half they fall down. In the next circle are represented the six realms of Saṁsāric existence beginning at the top and proceeding in a clockwise direction. They are the realms of gods, demi-gods,[35] hungry ghosts, hell beings, animals, men bound in turn by the twelve links of interdependent origination *paticca-samuppada*. Painting does illustrate such abstract concepts very forcefully and realistically.

Another class of *thankas* though of a religious nature was used as a good luck charm and hung in many homes to prevent the entry of evil spirits or displayed during events such as marriage, birth, death or changing a house as an amulet of protection. This was called the *rSipa-Ho* whose central figure was a big golden tortoise, the manifestation of Lord Mañjuśrī surrounded by flames as a protection against bad luck. On the stomach appear layers of circles with magic square numbers (*S Mewa d bu*) and eight trigrams *(Parkha Gay*). The five elements are represented on either sides, below the tail are the eight plants and at the bottom are written the sacred *mantras* inside the two 'wheels of *ngan pa kum thup*'. At the top are the depictions of the three gods Avalokiteśvara, Mañjuśrī and Vajrapāṇi. At the either sides of the *thanka* are symbols of serpents, earth spirits, gods and goddesses. Sacred symbols like *wangden* are also found.[36]

Medical paintings in particular the anatomy of the human body which helps in the understanding of bodily measurements and the branches of a tree which give the traditional Tibetan medical etiology in a symbolic form were also printed.

---

35. Detlef Ingo Lauf, *Tibetan Sacred Art,* 1976, p. 140.
36. Jhampa Kalsang, 'A Brief Introduction to rSipa-Ho' in *Tibetan Astronomy and Astrology — A Brief Introduction,* 1995, pp. 57-60.

Painting and the plastic arts

There are two types of paintings, mural painting and *thanka* paintings with the latter found in large numbers. Stylistically painting also follows the phases outlined in the case of *gompa*s and *chorten*s namely the early phase designated here as the Yarlung phase during which early Indian, particularly Gupta influences were discernible in addition to Nepalese, Khotanese and Central Asian influences. The second diffusion of Buddhism led to a spurt in the construction of monasteries but as far as painting was concerned new themes and influences had come, notably Kāśmīrī, which was highly popular in western Tibet and later, eastern Indian (Pāla-Sena) art with its developed Tāntric motifs. The fourteenth century inaugurated in Tibet a new type of art with the rise of the Sakyapas, later giving way to the regional styles such as the Lato school, Gyantse school and the Guge School finally culminating in a national style during the rule of the Dalai Lamas.[37]

Thankas

Thanka paintings are said to originate from the *paṭa-citra*s of ancient India, a form of visual aid and preaching employed effectively by the early Jaina and Buddhist preachers. *Paṭa-citras* were an effective supplement to the oral teachings, being light and portable, they could be rolled up and carried with the minimum of effort. Various sources trace the origin to Lord Buddha and one story goes this way that during the Buddha's lifetime, King Bimbisāra was given a gift of a priceless gem by King Udayana to which he wanted a substitute to return and finally requested the Lord Buddha whether he may have his picture done to which the great Master acquiesced. However the artist was filled with such bliss on seeing the Lord that he found it impossible to draw do anything. In the end the Buddha sat in front of a pool with the artist seeing the reflection on the water and finally

37. Jane Casey Singer, 'Early Thankas Eleventh-Thirteenth Centuries', Pratapaditya Pal, ed., *MARG,* vol. XLVIII, n. 1, p. 31.

reproducing a picture of the Lord.[38] Similar legends are found all of which trace the origin of painting to Bihar, which was the first area to exert style on Nepal and Tibet.[39] Mural paintings also have similar themes though differences exist about the treatment of subjects, the main difference is technical and also the purpose because *thankas* served multifarious motives.

Being a religious artefact, the preparation of a *thanka* was a religious duty, and it was necessary that the artist in most cases, was a lama artist trained in the *gompa* itself under the tutelage of a senior lama after having completed basic studies in Tibetan and having an inclination towards art. Art was not for art's sake at least with reference to those art forms partronised by the *gompa,* in short it was also a means of spiritual progress in the Buddhist path. Keeping in mind all these qualities, an artist was expected to be pure, devoted to his work, free of all bad influences, above all totally imbued with a sense of religiosity which should make him unconcerned about the monetary rewards.

Mistakes are not made easily by the artist as he got to paint after years of painstaking apprenticeship by learning to draw hands, legs and then ultimately the Buddha, the representative of an ideal being in a correct proportion prescribed by iconometric canons akin to the same measures used in the nine span construction of the *chorten.* So important were the religious restrictions that all paintings demanded certain levels of abstinence, particularly in the case of Avalokiteśvara and Tārā where the artist was not expected to imbibe alcohol, garlic, onions and meat.[40] The fearful guardian deities (*Srung-ma*) and tutelary deities (*yidam*) of which much has been extolled in fact demanded stricter preconditions from the artists such that he be an initiate of the particular class of Tantras because ordinary lay people could not be granted access to the sacred Tāntric lore

38. Mathew Kapsner, 'Thanka Painting', *Choyang,* n. 3, 1993, p. 17.
39. *Ibid.*, pp. 17-18.
40. *Ibid.,* p. 20.

disseminated only to the initiate which would otherwise lead to serious consequences. Like agricultural rituals that commence before the begining of the sowing season and building of a home, here also for a good and auspicious start sacred scriptures were read by a lama who then blessed the work place and then the artist. Such treatment of subjects and preconditions for painting were inevitably due to the *gompa* being the main patron.

Painting was done on a cloth surface that was painstakingly prepared and then stretched on a bamboo frame after which the whole surface was treated with glue and polished. Then the design is either sketched or transferred. After this, coats of paint were applied, then shading and outlining took place after which the *thanka* was given finishing touches. The process was in fact a detailed and cumbersome operation involving a substantial amount of artisanal labour for preparing the canvas to a good sense of calculation and geometry to sketch the figure very precisely according to rigid iconometry failing which the effectiveness of the *thanka* was negated. Application of colour in the right shades demanded an eye for detail and aesthetic sense which came after years of rigorous apprenticeship and practice. Finally the painting was completed and disengaged from the easel. This completed painting called *me-long* was sewn onto a coloured silk or brocade ribbon on all sides after which two rods were at the top (*thang-shing*) and another wooden rod at the bottom called *thong-thog* were joined to roll it which must always be done from below. A silken veil (*zhal khels*) was provided over the *thanka* to protect it from dust and smoke.

Symbolism played a definite role in the Tibetan religion and psyche finding expression at all levels of human creative activity, e.g., architecture and the various arts. The *maṇḍala* theory was adhered to in the field of painting too with sacred space being marked out from the profane, this worldly by a rainbow inasmuch as the wall of the temple (*cags-ri*). The rainbow was usually a tri-coloured one with red, yellow and blue. Like an entrance to the sacred realm, which is the gateway, here in a *thanka* a sky dragon was embroidered on brocade patch that is then fixed to the *thanka* indicative of an entrance. Pompousness was reflected in the gold burnishings done on the *thanka* after the application of shades and painting signifying a departure from the earlier simplicity. Precious stones and inflated larger than life sizes it was believed enhanced the value and merit of the patron.

Appliqued banners called *gos-sku,* literally translated as fabric image are an other example of Tibetan art evolving to the service of religion as ritual accompaniments designed the serve a religious purpose in a given social context. In 1468 the first Dalai Lama Gendun Trupa received an offering of 'bales of silk' out of which he conceived idea of making a *gos-sku* of the Śākyamuni in a gigantic size.[41] Menla Dhondup, a famous contemporary painter and artist was entrusted with this job which he competed at Tashilhunpo, producing the first ever *gos-sku* which after consecration by the first Dalai Lama brought forth good omens in the sky.[42]

Commonly made out a silk, pieces of cotton, yak leather were sewn on to a cloth to make a pattern or picture like a painting to which embroidery would be added for high-lighting the details. Fifteenth-century Tibet saw the apogee of architectural and artistic development which set a new style to be continued later on. This was also the period of Gelugpa consolidation over Tibet, the period when styles took shape to be continued later with very few modifications. The second *gos-sku* was made out of silk left over from the previous one, encrusted with two thousand seven hundred and seventy-five pearls and crystals to adorn Tārā. Menla Dhondup was a great innovator as he was conversant with the styles and designs, moreover he had a team of artisans who were always present in the workshops of the *gompa*s which churned out great quantities of *thanka*s. Gyantse, a monastic town was a famous centre of trade where Chinese

41. Valrae Reynolds, 'Fabric Images and Their special Role in Tibet' in Pratapaditya Pal, ed., *Marg,* vol. XLVIII, n. 1, p. 84.

42. *Ibid.*

and Nepalese influences were felt doubled up as one of the prime centres for the flowering of this art. Special mention must be made of the Kadampa monastery of Nas-rnying situated south-west of Gyantse which contained a Chinese scroll by which Menla Dhondup was impressed. Incidentally Newari craftsmen of Nepal also maintained long relations with this monastery, only going to show that monasteries had great interest in art as patrons of art, consumers of artefacts and this practice was also followed by individual living Buddha's, famous among such patrons were the abbots of Śākya. Another great patron was the prince of Gyantse, particularly the third prince Rabten Kunzang who commissioned a large appliqué banner depicting Śākyamuni, made out of three hundred and thirty bolts of cotton covered with silk on which thirty-seven people toiled for twenty-seven days.[43]

Art had many surrogate purposes, one of which we have already seen that it was a visual mode of preaching employed in ancient India. *Thanka* painting was a lineal successor to this art. It was put to multifarious use and the *gos-sku* was a continuation suited to the needs of the times. Large congegrations assembled at festivals and fairs held at the *gompa*s that were very auspicious events. Merit earning was one of the aims of life to which the Tibetan was oriented as we have seen in an earlier chapter, therefore, it was given religious sanction to this practice of viewing the holy *thanka*s and appliqué banners as 'Liberation through Sight' (Tib. *Mt' on grol*), a practice greatly appealing to folk sensibilities. The popularity of such practices can be gauged from the fact that some monasteries built sloping walls on the hillsides whereas others utilised the slopes of the hills if they were favourable geographically.[44]

Sculpture

Tibetan sculpture has produced vast number of specimens in

43. *MARG*, vol. XLVIII, p. 87.

44. *Ibid.*, p. 85.

metal but comparatively a minuscule quantity in stone and some items especially musical instruments where human bones were used though it is such examples that have hogged the limelight if one surveys the historiography of the early writings on Tibet. Butter sculpture and *torma* or ritual cakes made of flour (and may also he included in sculpture if we take the definition to its fullest and as a plastic art) were a peculiarity to Tibet and found nowhere else. Images of stucco provide another field of plastic arts enshrined in the *gompas*.

The subject-matter of sculpture was very much the same as painting sans colour (except in the butter sculptures) but with very mixed results. Painting, both mural and *thanka* have provided an artistic excellence, an element whose force was not fully expressed in sculpture limited as this art was by the same rigid iconometric rules prescribed for painting. Statues made their appearance in Buddhism at first during the period of Kaniṣka with the anthropomorphic representation of figures. Buddhism in its Tāntric form had grown vast enough to accommodate a pantheon derived in a greater part from Hindu Gods accommodated as tutelary deities and also in positions of not much eminence. Rituals were a mode of worship popular in the Tāntric way of worship, a set of practices to win over the malevolent spirits, also to gain magical power which was a historical development, in part an antithesis of early Buddhist principles. Results were, however, not very impressive in the field of iconography which could not scale great heights like paintings, limited by the greater technicalities involved in sculpture, where technical excellence weighed equally alongside artistic craftsmanship.

Examples of early Tibetan art betraying Indo-Nepalese post-Gupta influences manifested in the *tsuglag khang* of the so-called 'Cathedral of Lhasa' which had wood carvings dated around AD 641, i.e., the period of the 'First Diffusion of Buddhism', other examples were the temples of the Yarlung dynasty prominent among them is the Samye temple, Ramoche temple and the Tradruk monastery. The post-Gupta influences came via Nepal and it is this style that heavily influenced the early period. Statues were not very popular in the early period. The post-Langdarma period plagued Tibet into an anarchic situation which continued till AD 1000 roughly up to which time lack of stability and patronage did not witness any output of sculptures due to the slack demand. Buddhist revival in Guge inaugurated a new period. Some examples of the art of this period, like Tabo and Alchi have survived to this day. Michael Hess goes on to call the eleventh century as a golden age which is found in the high quality of artefacts styled elegantly and slender in shape marking itself off from the earlier stiff examples like the pillars at Jo-Khang in Lhasa.[45]

Kāśmīrī influence is quite easily discernible and also supported by literary evidence of Kāśmīrī craftsmen brought over to work on the western Tibetan *gompa*s. Wood, being plentiful in Kashmir the craftsmen excelled in this medium particularly at Alchi where the giant stuccos, pillars and even paintings show similar features as wood is more easy to carve on than stone giving room for intricacy.[46] Bronzes and wooden sculptures also abound but not in profusion though all of them share a common stylistic language which imparts a particular profile to the western Tibetan artefacts of this period. Buddha was still portrayed in the Gāndhāra style with inward looking eyes and an aquiline nose.

Strict iconometric guidelines followed by the artists made them copy the models which they did skillfully and at the same time absorbing influences from neighbouring countries compared to western Tibet which was open to Kāśmīrī influence and also isolated. Central and south Tibet were open to influences from Nepal through which Indian influences also percolated, in particular the Pāla art whose examples were in the Potala, Tashilhunpo monastery and Śākya monastery all of these like other big monasteries had store rooms to lock away old statues Pāla style was prevalent

45. Michael Hess 'Early Tibetan Sculpture' in Pratapaditya Pal, ed., *MARG,* vol. XLVIII, no. 4, p. 20.

46. David Snellgrove, n. 15, pp. 23-38.

all over Tibet, through it was not the exclusive one as we find central Asian Styles also co-existing, all these styles coming to Tibet by ways of pilgrims and traders. Distinctive mongoloid traces in face coupled with different (central Asian) forms of dress are the characteristics of these influences.

With the exception of Guge, which was isolated and later slipped into oblivion, central and southern Tibet comprising the Tibetan heartland can be said to have had a same style. Thirteenth-century statues of massive proportions executed in bronze of high quality in the Potala, Jo-Khang and Ramoche temples at Lhasa and Drangte monastery west of Gyantse show the great standards set in technique and style.

Tibetan art is essentially religious, from a functional viewpoint other accessories like the *phurbu* or magic dagger, the *vajra* (Tib. *dorje*), bells and beads all formed accompaniments of the ritual process which were made of metal and in addition were the beads and the prayer wheels, both a compulsory part of the monk and the layman's possessions without which his life would be incomplete. The *vajra* or the thunderbolt was one of the basic signifiers of esoteric rituals from which the name Vajrayāna Buddhism has come. Rich in symbolism the *vajra* too has embodied the concepts of peaceful and wrathful gods symbolised by the style of spokes, with those of the peaceful one meeting at the tip and those of the wrathful gods slightly splayed at the tip.[47] The number of spokes is nine, five or three like the rigid rules of the iconometric process. In the nine-spoked *vajra,* the upper spokes symbolise the Buddhas of the five families and the four mothers, one between each of the Buddhas while the lower spokes represent the five wisdom's and four immeasurable wishes of love, compas-sion, equanimity and joy. In the case of the five-spoked *vajra* the upper sets of the five spokes symbolise the five wisdom's. The sea monstresses mouth from which each spoke emerge represents freedom from cyclic existence, ultimate goal of Buddhism. Likewise the two lotuses at the hub of the *vajra,* the upper one

47. 'The Vaira Bell and Beads', *Choyang,* vol. 2, 1987, p. 79.

symbolises the eight *bodhisattvas* while the lower lotus symbolises the eight goddesses.

The bell called *dribul* (Skt. *ghaṇṭā*) is virtually inseparable from the *vajra* for ritual purposes and it has no independent function, therefore, it is usually paired with a *vajra*. Not one aspect of the bell is free of symbolism, which is worked out to the last detail reflecting the precision and complexity of rituals. The round base of the bell has a vase above it on which is the face of the goddess Prajñāpāramitā, inside is the nectar of accomplishment above which is a lotus, a moon disc and finally a *vajra*. The lotus has eight petals four of which symbolise the four mothers and the other four symbolise the four goddess. The interior hollow of the bell symbolises the wisdom cognising emptiness that is further elucidated by the clapper supposed to represent the sound of emptiness.[48] The *vajra* and bell are always joined and represent method and wisdom respectively and have an undivided unity and, therefore, never employed separately.

Beads were an essential part of the religious rhythm and in Tibetan Buddhism they were used to appease, increase, overcome or tame by forceful means. Rosaries for each of the above-mentioned purposes were made of different materials, they were of crystal, mother of pearl, pearl. In white or clear colour and the beads had to number hundred and were generally used to clear obstacles and other calamities.[49] Beads used to increase life span, knowledge and merit should be made of gold, silver, copper or lotus seeds and number a hundred and eight. A small rosary of twenty-five beads made from a compound of ground sandalwood, saffron and other fragrant substances served to overcome or tame others, but the underlying intention should be for the welfare of all sentient beings and just not simply for selfish motives. Extremely malevolent spirits whose figure in sculptural and poetic representation find a place here with beads made of *rakṣā* seeds or human bones numbering sixty tied with nine

---

48. *Choyang*, vol. 2, 1987, p. 80.

49. *Ibid.*

strings (all beads were tied with nine strings in a rosary) serving the purpose.[50] But such examples are rare and ceremonies also scarce in number, here the malevolent spirits visualised as a black dense ball. Altruistic motives were the key word and the last mentioned rosary could only be used by a *bodhisattva* who was extremely motivated by compassion while praying with the rosary the symbolism helped in keeping the adherent reminded of the ends one should aspire for and when the nine threads of the bead symbolise Buddha Vajradhara and the eight *bodhisattvas*, the large bead at the end stood for wisdom which cognised emptiness and the cylindrical head surmounting it stood for emptiness itself, both symbolise having vanquished all opponents.

Tibetan butter sculpture and tormas

The art of making sculptures out of butter was peculiar to Tibet and was centered on the *gompa* as also the art of *torma* making both of which were indispensable during the annual festivals. Both butter sculptures and ritual cakes or *torma* had a base of leather to support the outer plastering of butter on which the whole artistry was worked out. The large pieces of leather were first glued on to a wooden frame in shapes of triangular pyramids, a shape common to both butter sculptures and ritual cakes. Made entirely of butter they were periodically dipped in cold water to lend it firmness. On the cakes some of which may be massive in size of two storeys height due to the Tibetan's fondness of grandeur had large surfaces where the sculptures were fitted in. The eight auspicious symbols, the seven emblems of a universal monarch, a *garuḍa,* lion, tiger or dragon were the most popular motifs being represented on the sculptures.[51]

There was no scriptural convention regarding the selection of themes or measurements and artists were free to modify and innovate. Famous butter sculptures were done by the

---

50. *Choyang*, vol. 2.
51. 'Tibetan Butter Sculpture', *Choyang*, vol. 1, no. 2, 1987, p. 98.

Gyumed Tāntric College whose favourite compositions included Tsongkhapa seated formally or riding on a horse, an elephant or the eight Indian *paṇḍitas*.[52] Designs and motifs ranged from simple to complex and colourful such as the Guhya-samāja *maṇḍala* a complex motif made of small pieces of rounded butter in various colours. In contrast the Buddhas of the five families, the sixteen *arhats* in caves and so forth was considered simple. The first Tibetan month, the auspicious time when the Buddha defeated his six principal opponents was considered to be auspicious and on the fifteenth of the month on the full moon day there were great festivities, like the Great Prayer Festival, the monastic confession, and the usual exhibitory debates. On this day, the Bakhor the area around the Jo-khang, a half mile in length was lined with butter sculptures made by the different colleges of Drepung, Sera, Ganden, the two Tāntric colleges in Lhasa several monasteries and aristocratic families Exhibition of these sculptures started late in the hours of the afternoon and after viewing by the monks, the public were allowed to view.

The ritual cakes on the other hand were part of a ritual to quell evil, triangular in shape and made of butter, red-coloured and encircled by flames, they were all set to be thrown on to a tent of straw to be burnt later.[53] Various *gompas* brought their own ritual cakes in a procession, the monks dressed in a warlike manner. After reading the verses the ritual master announced that these are the symbols of wrathful forces inimical to the government of Tibet, its people and the Buddhist religion and therefore they should be sent back to where they came from. The philosophy underlying this is that the spirits cannot be tamed and need to be destroyed which is done out of compassion as the ritual master prays that in the next life the spirits may gain a favourble rebirth.

---

52. 'Tibetan Butter Sculpture', *Choyang*, vol. 1, no. 2, 1987.

53. 'The Throwing of Ritual Cakes', *Choyang*, vol. 1, no. 2, 1987, p. 93.

Conclusion

The *gompas* were the primary patrons and repositories of art in pre-modern Tibet with an endless list of subject-matter ranging from the Buddha, *bodhisattvas*, Tārās, *mahāsiddhas*, *arhats*, Great Indian and Tibetan Masters. Buddhist motifs like the wheel of life, *rSipa-Ho,* medicinal *thankas*, *maṇi* walls ritual accessories and *kaṅkaṇīs* (gateways). Influences in art came in the early stage from India and Nepal and later from China and central Asia which were readily incor-porated showing the dynamism in religion and styles. Primarily sacred art, monastic art and architecture performed a wide variety of functions mainly of a religious nature. Paintings were useful for both meditation and to a lesser degree in medicine. Above all art served as an instrument to ward off the spirits of which the average Tibetan lived in constant dread of.

Monastic architecture followed the great tradition of Tibetan society thus integrating vast parts of the Tibetan culture areas by using the same cultural language in construction. Incorporation of earlier pre-Buddhist deities and other tutelary deities also served to this end. The early base of art and architecture with Indian influences gave way to later Chinese influences and during this inter-regnum, arose various schools of painting which ultimately developed into a national style during the reign of the Dalai Lamas.

5

Socio-Economic Role of the Gompa

THE second diffusion of Buddhism leading to its establishment as the state religion under the patronage of the religious kings gave Buddhism the centre stage in Tibetan society and polity. The fall of the apostate Langdarma signalled the end of a historical period in Tibetan history. The resultant chaos and anarchy continued for around five centuries with an altogether new picture emerging on the aftermath, the emerging rule of the monasteries relegating the royalty behind the scenes. Monastic influence permeated all levels of Tibetan society, be it, economics or art and most important of all the changed mindset of the people who were imbued with a deep sense of religiosity manifesting itself not only in the spiritual but also the mundane life and the material, conditioning the choices (so crucial to the study of economics) and virtually reordering the societal pattern.

Economies, even in modern society bear imprints of cultural language of a particular unit of social organisation (nation, caste, tribe, etc.) which condition the choice thereby proving the fallacy that economics is an abstract science universally applicable wholesale. Historical developments in Tibetan society under the overarching influence of the *gompa* led to the process where all facets of society had religious input in some varying degree. Thus, when we talk of economy and society in relation to *gompa* we are only seeing the economic aspects which are part of an intricate whole so inextricably intertwined that we have to constantly keep referring to the socio-religious context every now and then as Tibet is a classic example of a society whose dynamics cannot be explained by just numbers.

At the outset two things need to be stressed while speaking on the socio-economic system of the *gompas*. One is the paucity of source material and the second is the diversity of Tibetan society. Sources are mainly gleanings from travelogues of the missionaries, to later explorers of the nineteenth and twentieth centuries, in addition to information gathered from Tibetan refugees. Problems encountered here are some contradictory data, generalisations about the nature of society and above all an ethnocentric bias. The diversity of Tibetan society has prompted writers like Geoffrey Samuel to speak of societies[1] rather than a single society, reason being the marked differences in the way of life and social organisation in central Tibet, western Tibet, eastern Tibet and the nomads of ChangTang to which one many add the monastic society which itself was a society within a society albeit an alternative form of social arrangement.[2]

In pre-modern Tibet, the Central Government of the Dalai Lama based at Lhasa, the *gompas* and the nobility were the three taxing authorities who held possession of the productive resources, i.e., land and capital and taxed the subjects within their respective jurisdictions by virtue of their superordinate position within their respective spheres thereby regulating the economic life of the 'subjects'.[3] The whole of the Tibetan population therefore fell into either of these two classes the taxing authorities comprising of the above-mentioned classes of monastic society and nobility, the rest were the taxpayers of whom the bulk were agriculturists and nomads with some exceptions like the traders whom we shall see in detail.

---

1. Geoffrey Samuel, *Civilized Shamans Buddhism in Tibetan Societies*, 1993, p. 3.
2. Melvyn Goldstein and Paljor Tsarong 'Tibetan Buddhist Monasticism: Social, Psychological and Cultural Implications', *The Tibet Journal*, vol. 10, no. 1, spring 1985, pp. 14-17.
3. Ugen Gombo, 'The Traditional Tibetan Economy an overbview analysis from a socio-anthropological.perspective', *Tibetan Review*, February to March 1978, vol. 13, p. 20.

Historical evolution of the Tibetan society

The Tibetan society is a union of races, united by a common culture and language and above all an adaptation to an ecology which led to interlinkages between different segments of the society. The myth of the Tibetans descending from the union of a monkey and a mountain ogress best illustrates this myth of the union of races.[4] Such origin myths are part of world folklore, the main actors or symbols in the myths being totems or tutelary deities. From an anthropological point of view, the origin of the Tibetans is located among the non-Chinese Chiang tribes, though studies on the physical anthropology and linguistics of Tibet is lacking, it would be safe to assert this conclusion keeping in mind the existing body of knowledge.

The union of various Tibetan tribes saw the rise of the first ever kingdom on the Yarlung river basin which has been the base of Tibetan history, as all earlier classical works tend to centre on this river valley as a cradle of civilizations. Buddhism was introduced into Tibet in AD 630 and the later events are too well known to the recounted here. Suffice to say that the surplus producing Yarlung river valley with its centralised empire encompassing the whole of Tibet was beset with internal strife owing to Bonpo-Buddhist rivalry. The emergent picture is one of chaos with independent states vying for power that finally inaugurated an era of monastic rule relegating the nobility to the background.

Monasteries became the chief centres of political and military power controlling the resources of the country. A turning point in Tibetan history came with the reform movement started by Tsongkhapa, eventually paving way for the dominance of the Gelugpa (yellow hat sect). Tibet was once again under the control of a Central Government at Lhasa. The earlier kings officials and holders of estates formed the nobility.

---

4. David Snellgrove and Hugh Richardson, *A Cultural History of Tibet*, 1968, rpt., p. 21.

In an earlier chapter, we had seen the classification of Tibetan communities into centralised agricultural communities, remote agricultural community pastoral communities and urban communities. By far the largest component of Tibetan society can be classified under centralised agricultural communities. They were centered in the major river valleys which was the base to generate a surplus as there was enough land to yield a good agricultural return. Main characteristics of the centralised Tibetan villages were a striking link between their distribution and the power of the Central Government. The Yarlung river valley comprising the administrative areas of Ü and Tsang had the largest concentration of these settlements all forming part of the Central Government of Dalai Lama. Other productive areas included enclaves in the Hor and Derge states in the east, in Bhutan and also in Ladakh. Incidentally the highest concentration of the *gompa*s was found in these areas as they had a strong resource base.[5] The resources were managed and appropriated by the large estates owned by the aristocratic families, Central Government, *gompa*s and individual lamas (the last two have been grouped together). The household was the basic building block in this type and social formation that showed a high degree of stratification. So important was the household as a unit that all property belonged not to the head of the family but to the household and the relation of the taxing authority was to the household and not to the family.[6] The households along with economic obligations all passed down through the male line.

Full members of the village were called *drongpa* and belonged to a household bearing its name and in their capacity as taxpayers were called *tre'ba.*[7] Below the *tre'ba* were

---

5. In chapter 1, 'Geographical Location and Origin of the Saṁgha', a map showing the distribution of the *gompa*s is given which illustrates in graphic detail the above assertion.
6. Charles Bell, *The People of Tibet*, 1991, p. 84.
7. Thomas T. Wiley, 'Macro Exchanges: Tibetan Economics and the Roles of Politics and Religion', *The Tibet Journal,* vol. XI, no. 1, Spring 1986, p. 5.

another group ranked socially lower in status called *duchung* (literally small smoke).[8] In contrast to the *tre'ba,* the *duchung* did into possess any permanent land rights and generally worked as tenants on the *drongpa* farms with others eking out a living as itinerant labourers. The above-mentioned categories constituted the vast majority of the population in the agricultural areas being a vital element in the production process, together collectively being classified as *miser*, a term open to various interpretations ranging from 'commoner' to 'serf', both of which involve larger questions concerning society and politics.

All households in a village generally belonged to an estate allotted to any of the three taxing authorities who imposed the taxes on the households which had been allotted to them in addition to many corvee obligations. Land was inheritable as long as the *drongpa* households kept their tax and corvee payments regularly to the respective taxing authority. Apart from the taxes and corvee obligations on individual *tre'ba* households, there were some taxes and labour obligations which the whole village had to collectively fulfil. Taxes and corvee obligations weighed heavily on the *tre'ba* than on the *duchung* whose tax services were corvee only. The status of the *duchung* could have originated from their being not a part of the original village community but as settlers who were always accorded less proprietary rights. This could have been the reason for their lower social status. In all clarity, it must be said that they were not untouchables. The *misers* were classified as government *miser*, *miser* of the aristocratic estate or *miser* of the monastic estates. After fulfilling the obligation to the aristocratic or the monastic estates[9] in their particular cases, they also had to fulfil some special obligations to the Central Government. This social formation was the most numerous and had the highest productivity in terms of surplus, followed by remote agricultural communities

8. Geoffrey Samuel, n. 1, p. 118.

9. Surkhang Wangchen Gelek, 'Government Monastic and Private Taxation in Tibet', *The Tibet Journal*, vol. X, no. 1, spring 1986, p. 21.

which were a modified and watered down version of the above due to scarce resource base after which came the nomadic way of life, an altogether different form of production, all of which were a part of the production process in the Tibetan socio-economic field.

A direct observation that the *miser* was burdened with too much of tax and labour obligations on account of the fact that the centralised agricultural communities had good scope for agricultural surplus due to fertility of the land and abundant water. The tax paying *tre'ba* and the corporate estate holders were the dynamic classes in Tibetan society according to Ugen Gombo.

Aristocrats were called *gerpa* and the *ponpo,* or *dzongpon* (Lord of the estate), came from this class which was the main supplier of officials to the government, had independent estates farmed by the *miser*. Society was not watertight, there being instances of *tre'ba* who were more wealthy than the aristocrats and in course of time entered this strata.[10] Remnants of old ruling families, part of the nobility holding high administrative posts hereditarily like the nobility of Saskya[11] or the chieftains of semi-independent states, comprised the aristocracy. One could also become an aristocrat by recognition of the services he rendered to the Government but such cases were rare.

The *ngagpa* were another group of people like the aristocrats who belonged to hereditary lama families and were on a high social scale like the aristocrats. Like the aristocrats, the hereditary lama families were also owners of estates.[12] Social mobility was there among the families of *tulku*s and most in the case of the Dalai Lama's family, reason being their association with the *gompa* and religion. The process works in a way that the family of a Dalai Lama gets an estate

---

10 . Melvyn. C. Goldstein, 'Reexamining Choice, Dependency and Command in the Tibetan Social System, Tax Appendages and other Landless Serfs', *The Tibet Journal,* vol. XI, no. 4, Winter 1986, p. 91.

11. C.W. Casinelli and Robet B. Ekvall, *A Tibetan Principality, The political system of Saskya*, 1969, pp. 214-19.

12. Charles Bell, n. 6, p. 66.

and his family members are accommodated in the aristocracy similarly reincarnate lamas and their families formed part of this class. At the bottom of the hierarchy were the *Yawa,* a despised class with whom matrimonial and commensual connections were regarded degrading, hence they were a class to be avoided. They were otherwise referred to as the 'impure bones'.

The *miser*'s rights, duties and obligations were inherited as soon as he or she attained the age of thirteen, a tax was levied which went on till the person reached the age of sixty after which there was redemption from the tax. Avenues for mobility were many in Tibet both legally and quasi-legally. Many *miser*s were well to do sometimes even equalling the wealth of the aristocratic families which only demonstrated the great differences in the composition of the *miser*s who could not be taken as a homogeneous class, both socially and economically. However, for those prosperous *miser*s aspiring to become part of the aristocracy, one way was to enter into matrimonial relations with them.[13]

Monastic wealth consisted of lands, herds of livestock, money and barely, out of which land had the greatest importance in the order of productivity and returns and also the largest share in the above items. The reason is not difficult to fathom for the biggest monasteries were located in the centralised agricultural zones which were favourable eco-zones providing a good surplus base. Monasteries were either wholly absent in the nomadic areas or were of small size not large enough to be comparable with the ones located in the favourable eco-zones. Buildings, *thanka*s, idols, etc., completed the list of movable and immovable assets.

Land supposed to have been held by the monasteries is not exactly known. Land granted to the monasteries was tax-free, diverting a great part of the income from ending in the coffers of the state considering the percentage of land held we can safely assume that the monasteries commanded

---

13. Melvyn. C. Goldstein, n. 10. pp. 90-3.

enormous resources. Figures from Ladakh in the extreme west give a clearer picture. Hemis the biggest *gompa* of Ladakh was also the richest, endowed with fifty-one villages.[14] It was Ralpachen the Buddhist king who first started the practice of endowing monasteries with land. Yeshe Ö presented Rinchen Zangpo with an estate in Purang, another instance of endowment.[15] Since then all endowments and further land accruing to the *gompas* were on paper with clear title deeds as land ownership could often lead to disputes. The process of land acquisition by a *gompa* could be achieved by granting of villages or estate by the Central Government to the monastery for endowment after which the land was farmed. Donations of pieces of land by individual households to the monastic estates were another method of acquisition. As the household was the basic unit of social organisation, some households did not have a heir or lineal descendant to continue the family line and in many cases donated their land and livestock to the monastery. Parents of terminally ill children also vowed to donate their entire property to the monastery if the child got well, thus increasing the wealth of the monasteries. It was not always necessary that the land be allotted to the monastery. We find many precedents of land being alienated for the use of the Khamtsens. The *labrangs* also had property ranging from as low as a single room in a *gompa to* vast tracts of land almost equalling the size of a *dzong.*[16] As we have seen that the monasteries had been delegated powers by the state to levy tax, agriculture was a paying proposition with labour being easily mobilized under the system where *miser* were attached to the estates as tenants. The monasteries also granted land for housing purposes to the households on payment of adequate compensation. The monastic estates including *labrangs* are

---

14. O.C. Handa, *Buddhist Monasteries in Himachal Pradesh*, 1987, p. 130.

15. *The Blue Annals*, p. 68.

16. Paljor Tsarong, *Economy and Ideology in a Tibetan Monastic Estate in Ladakh: Process of Production, Reproduction and Transformation,* Ph.D. Thesis, 1993, p. 23.

called *chos-gzhis* and the land holdings of the major *labrang*s fall in the range of three hundred *don*s while the medium ones possesed about twenty *don*s. For those *labrang*s, which were poorly endowed with just a small tenement or a room in the *gompa,* it could not be considered as a viable economic unit. There was only one crop of barley sown in the summer and harvested in spring. The men did sowing while both sexes participated in harvesting the grain. The tax was around 1/5 to 1/6 of the produce according to Charles Bell. Peas and buckwheat along with some rice were cultivated but only in some areas that were close to the southern border and had a salubrious climate, but barley dwarfed the other grains in terms of net sown area and acreage. Due to religious sanctions, land was not mined in Tibet while in parts of Mongolia the lands of the Gelugpa Order's were used profitably for coal mining.[17]

Next to land, the herds of the monastery were another productive asset providing the *gompa* with butter, an indispensable ingredient in the preparation of tea, that was used to moisten *tsampa,* the staple diet of Tibet. Yak and sheep were the biggest component along with *dzo,* a hybrid animal. The *drog-pa* or nomads grazed in the northern plains of ChangTang where only grass grew, in addition to using vast stretches of uncultivated pasture land in the south and the eastern parts of the country. Like land, cattle were also donated to the monasteries depending on the fame and ability of the *gompa* to attract donations. Cattle population increased year after year, which was sold by the nomads and much counted as a prime investment for farmers and monasteries that could afford them. Grazing was to take place on the specific land allotted to the respective taxing authorities overseen by a government official called *shes-dpon* who looked after many cattle belonging to *gompa*s. Trespass on government land by aristocratic and monastic cattle was punishable by fine payable to the nearest *shes-dpon.*[18] Tax

17. Robert James Miller, *Monasteries and Culture Change in Inner Mongolia,* 1959, pp. 103-4.
18. Surkhang Wangchen Gelek, n. 9, p. 33.

arrangements showed regional variations but by and large the monastic and aristocratic establishments followed a system called *skye-yod'chi-yod,* under which one *khal* of butter for every male yak and two *khal* of butter from each female yak was taken in taxation.[19] Tax was levied on the original number of cattle whose census was taken every year with an allowance of one-tenth of the number given as deprecation. The natural increase exceeding the census could be kept by the nomads.

Bum-pa Bib blugs was another system of taxation of aristocratic and monastic nomads that was more liberal as allowances and wages was generous. All butter, yak hair and leather directly went to the monasteries or the aristocratic owners respectively.[20] Nomads coming under this system did not have to account for, or substitute the cattle and it had been observed that those who came under this system possessed a large number of cattle. Only in Mongolia, a predominantly pastoral country did herds of cattle outweigh land in terms of monastic resources, but the composition of herds there was slightly different with the absence of yaks and sheep, oxen and horses comprising the largest numbers. Tibetan wool was famous from the period of the Yuans, therefore, it emerged as a commodity of trade which only went towards investment in sheep. Later, in the eighteenth and nineteenth centuries the fame of Tibetan wool reached Europe and large wool marts emerged in Ladakh and Kalimpong.[21] Animals were used for transportation, a vital lifeline in a country that did not have any wheeled form of transport.

Wealth in terms of money accrued to the *gompa* from taxes, when not paid in kind and mainly from donations. Donations were a major source of revenue right from the days of the early Buddhist *saṁgha* as the *saṁgha* was dependent on the laity for support right from its inception.

---

19. Surkhang Wangchen Gelek, n. 9, p. 34.
20. *Ibid.*
21. Charles Bell, n. 6, p. 117.

Theoretically and also in early Buddhism, before it become a cenobital form of living, monks had to go and beg for food and alms daily, a practice which even now continues in the South East Asian countries which follow Theravāda Buddhism. In Tibet, the monks went out on a fund-raising drive for a specific purpose such as the conduct of particular rituals or building of monasteries for which the people subscribed according to their economic condition and keeping in mind the fame of the monastery, this form of subscription was called *jinda*.[22] Another form of subscription was customary for the conduct of rituals, some of which involved huge sums of money. Li-An Che gives an example from a field study done at Labrang monastery about a festival for which meals had to be provided for fifteen days which worked out in dollar terms to $46,710 in the 1930s. This ambit of operation consisted of thirteen villages and each tribe's turn came once in thirteen years and hence the responsibility was not annual and dispersed over a period of time.[23]

Loans given by the monastery and the *labrang*/living Buddhas were another source of economic gain for the monastery. Money-lending was perfectly in consonance with the religious tenets, there being no sanctions against it. The rates of interest were 10 per cent to 15 per cent and in many cases the interest was being repaid every year but the principle could not, so finally the interest collected exceeded the principle itself.[24] All sections of the population took loans on interest for some specific purpose, which were more or less non-productive. It was estimated that a great percentage of Lhasan nobles took loans on interest, how many of them to invest in trade is not know. Trade was one of the dynamic areas of Tibet's economy registering an increase year after year as it afforded mobility, financial independence, adventure and above all it was tax free, thus traders were

---

22. Giuseppe Tucci, *Tibet: Land of Snows*, J.E. Stapleton Driver, tr., 1967, rpt., p. 97.
23. Chie Nakne, ed., Li-An Che, *Labrang A study in the field*, 1982, p. 7.
24. Jampel Khalden, 'Interest Rates in Tibet', *The Tibet Journal*, vol. 1, no. 1, 1975, pp. 109-11.

the main creditors of the monasteries and the Living Buddhas. Both the *gompas* and the Living Buddhas indulged in trade, all of which must have led to the generalisation that Tibetans are born traders confusing the dynamic element in Tibetan economy as a universal trend. This also goes to show the other view portraying Tibetan society being static, landlocked and self-sufficient as invalid.[25]

Wool was the most coveted item traded to both China and India but largely to India, especially the great woolmarts of Kalimpong and Ladakh in the eastern and western parts of the Himālayas. Other products having a market in India were rock salt, produce of the northern plains where it occurred on the beds and banks of lakes. Yak-tails were another item used in Hindu temples. The trade routes to China went from Gansu in Kham and Szechwan carrying silk, horses and yak-meat. Caravans also went to Mongolia carrying yak-meat incense for prayer worship and copies of the Tibetan holy books, the *Kangyur* and *Tangyur.*[26] Imports were tea in substantial quantities from China, rice from Nepal and Bhutan, some cotton and musk from India. The balance of trade was always in favour of Tibet's balance the exception being China. Traders were of two kinds, the local traders who brought small items and displayed it in the villages where people come to watch out of and not to buy. The other type of large-scale trading was the area in which the monasteries, living Buddha's, the aristocrats took part in. Such traders travelled in caravans with a retinue of servants, always fearful of bandits and warlike tribes such as the Goloks and other peoples in the Khams. Two caravans went to Mongolia every year, each of them being joined by pilgrims both in need of mutual security accompanied by *dobdobs* or monastic police. The economic surplus of grain, livestock and salt was the main factor that spurred trade.

It is not known whether the *gompa* envinced any interest in the local internal trade that was anyway not on such an

25. David MacDonald, *Cultural Heritage of Tibet*, 1978, rpt., p. 124.
26. Charles Bell, n. 6, p. 123

organised scale as the international trade. Local trade was handled by the Tsong-pa, a mercantile class who came from the poorest of the families for whom trade afforded upward mobility.[27] But such trade was absolutely necessary in Tibet due to the geographical situation which dictated two ways of life, the pastoral and the agricultural with none-being equally self-sufficient and both dependent on the products of the others, viz., salt, butter and meat with barley on the other spectrum. According to Ekvall

> the dependence of the two groups on trading has fostered the development of trade routes, determined the seasonal movement of trade, created systems of value, and set patterns of behaviour in trade associations.[28]

*Gompa*s and living Buddha's had huge resources of cash which needed an outlet for investment and trade offered the best alternative as it guaranteed high returns with comparatively less hassles because the market for goods of export and import were fixed. Trade also required less manpower than agriculture, which itself was a big problem. Lack of any another avenues like handicrafts which were only in a preliminary stage, an example of which were the small factories of Lhasa, hampered venues for investment. For the religious-minded, Tibetan Buddhism did not impose any negative sanctions against trade, but on the contrary the rise of the trading community in India during the Buddha's period and their active patronage of the Buddhist religion endeared Buddhism to the traders. According to the *Vinaya,*[29] the rules of the *saṁgha,* monks were not supposed to indulge in any trade or vocation that held good for the monastery too, but here in the Tibetan context we see they

---

27. Eva Dargyay, *Tibetan Village Communities: Structure and Change*, 1982, p. 77 in Leonard R. Chapela 'Economic Institutions of Buddhist Tibet', *The Tibet Journal*, vol. 17, no. 3, Autumn 1992, p. 17.

28. Robert Ekvall, *Religious Observances in Tibet: Patterns and Functions*, 1964, p. 192 in Leonard R. Chapela, n. 27. p. 20.

29. *Vinaya Texts, Cullavagga*, V.28, 1.

were ignored. It is noteworthy that the luxury items of India and China were not traded in Tibet. The reason was not that the people could not afford them but the frugality and mental conditioning did not care much for this. An average Tibetan's possessions were meager, which included two pairs of dresses, one for daily use, the other being kept for wearing on festive occasions. Similarly household utensils and items were kept to the barest minimum, while on the expenditure side, a good sum of money and commodities were given to the monasteries for reasons which we shall analyse later. Luxury goods in essence were adornments and fashion items whose use the ordinary Tibetan believed was not good. According to popular superstition, any sudden change in mode of dress and adornments was a sign of ominous portents for the future. Among the properties of the *gompa,* Miller lists the living Buddha as economic asset of the monastic system in Mongolia.[30] The arguments he advances to support this are fairly convincing and can be applied even in the Tibetan context. The name of a living Buddha carried weight, as there were upwards of ten thousand *tulku*s in old Tibet. Their special schooling excellence, charisma all led to the attraction of disciples from far and wide. Contributions were made to the *gompa* as an institution for some specific purpose or endowments particularly to the living Buddha. These donations were called as *lisnyen-Gkun* or help homage offerings and were of outmost economic relevance considering the very large proportion of wealth from the secular control and utilisation to an individual *lama* or religious organisations with minimum solicitation unlike the contributions which were solicited by the monastery for repairs and other works, but very much like offerings which implied an element of merit. Monastic life was the ideal of the Buddhist philosophy but since all people could not become monks, the sponsoring of monks and the monasteries, particular rituals itself was an act that earned religious merit, the accumulation of which would help in getting a favourable rebirth in the next life.

Merit was accumulated by donations (Skt. *dāna*) a

30. Robert James Miller, n. 17, p. 91.

practice prevalent from the days of Buddha having both an economic and a religious meaning since its inception.[31] From an economic viewpoint the concentration of wealth in the hands of a few leads to relative deprivation, resulting in poverty which breeds hatred. The social explanation of this according to Buddhist morality and ethics is that the individual strives for his happiness only rather than for the happiness of the whole society which would be ideal (*bahujanahitāya*). *Dāna*, therefore, performed the role of economic redistribution of wealth. The accumulation of merit was to ensure a good rebirth enabling the layman to finally break out the cycle of birth and rebirth so central to the theory of Buddhism, a theory very deeply ingrained in the Buddhist mind.

Medicinal treatment by the *gompa*s and the doctors (*amchi*s) also brought in additional endowments. But at times medicine would fail leaving no respite for the patient whose only hope was to appease the supernatural for which some paintings called *rSipa-Ho* were commissioned. *Thangka* paintings and copies of *Kangyur* and *Tangyur,* the Tibetan religious texts printed at the famous monastery of Narthang were commissioned, thus pointing to transference of wealth.[32] One of the reasons why the category of food and non-food products in the economic life of Tibet has not been adopted here is because categorising peasants and herdsmen on one side and the monks on the other end of the spectrum would imply that the latter were consumers only. Far from it monks worked as painters, artists, calligraphers, and providers of ritual services and also as astrologers.

From the cradle to the grave, the service of a monk was indispensable as the new born child's horoscope was to be drawn up, the necessary rituals for ploughing, family rituals such as placating evil spirits, giving lucky charms or conducting rituals for the prosperity of the individual and

---

31. *Vinaya Texts, Kulllavagga* V.1, 3, gives an instance of *seṭṭhi* erecting buildings for the *bhikku*s.

32. Alexandra David Neel, *Magic and Mystery in Tibet*, 1993, rpt., p. 71.

the household. Marriage and finally death also involved rituals having regional variations and the strength of beliefs ranging from minimal services among the nomads to whom the religious missions went to every year conducting rituals for the deceased during that particular year, to ward off hail and snow, the excess of which could even wipe out entire herds of animals in a span of a week. Ladakhis on the other hand patronised the lamas much more, taking their services for rituals, which were very occasional in the village.[33] To gauge the high volume of socio-economic participation in the religious affairs, a short statistical survey would help throw light. Tibet had twenty thousand farming communities and if we include Ladakh, which also falls in the category of centralised agricultural areas the number would rise substantially. Dingri about which much has been studied comes under the category of remote agricultural community where surplus was not of the same magnitude as the centralised areas but whose *gompa*s never lacked funds though small in size as the munificence of the laity was a pan-Tibetan phenomenon. Tibetans spent roughly 50 per cent of their post-tax incomes on religious affairs,[34] the lions share of which went to the *gompa*s and the living Buddha's apart from the unorthodox lamas who formed a minuscule minority indicates that it is first more than formal economics which is in play. First, the *miser* and the aristocratic family would not have to incur such a debt and secondly, if the debts were there, they could minimise on the religious expenses and clear off their debts, both of which were not followed. Most Tibetans especially the commoners and monks led a frugal life concerned only with the bare necessities. Even the aristocrats did not have many avenues to spend. Thus, the Tibetan psyche was neither fully neither mystic nor entirely this worldly but had three orientations, the *bodhi* orientation, the *karma* orientation and the pragmatic orientation.

---

33. Tsering Shakya, Tashi Rabgyas and John Crook, 'Monastic Economics in Zangskar, 1980', in Crook and Osmaston, ed., *Himalayan Buddhist Villages*, 1996, pp. 609, 628-9.

34. Leonard R. Chapela, n. 27, p. 11.

After meeting the bare necessities of life, came the *karma* and *bodhi* orientations, the agendas of concern for the average individual which was to do good and earn merit. Accumulation of wealth and food (barley) was singly due to the frugal and spartan lifestyle of the monks which led to the larders being full and in cases of crop failure people came for barley loan. It is notable that in Tibet throughout the course of her history there was never any agrarian revolt or famine.[35]

Gompas like the north monastery at Saskya steadfastly stuck to the *Vinaya* code that prohibited any commercial role. *Gompas* such as these became famous for their piety and it is, therefore, not appropriate to label all the *gompas* as economic functionaries.[36] A considerable number of *gompas* were located in remote agricultural communities which exhibited a common feature, i.e., a close association of the *gompa* with farming community and farming operations. Typically each *gompa* had a major sponsor who was a village community, also forming the recruitment ground for the new monks. Bigger *gompas* like Hemis in Ladakh had 51 revenue villages under its jurisdiction, all of which were not directly affiliated to the main *gompa* but looked after, by the daughter houses located in the particular village.[37] Mother houses at times transferred villages from the jurisdiction of one *gompa* to another. Disputes over jurisdiction of the villages was an issue of discord amongst *gompas* as they provided the material basis of sustenance, viz., barley, livestock, milk, cheese and other products apart from labour contributed by the laity and monks for the *gompas*. The eldest son stayed on to continue the family line and household while the younger

35. Franz Michael, 'Traditional Tibetan Polity and its Potential for Modernization', *Tibet Journal,* vol. XI, no. 4, Winter 1986, p. 75. Also see Tsepon W.D. Shakalpa, *Tibet — A Political History*, 1988, rpt., p. 4.
36. C.W. Casinellin, n. 11, pp. 292. ff.
37. Dr. Harjeet Singh, *Ladakh — Problem of Regional Developmnet in the context of Growth Point Strategy,* Ph.D. Thesis, 1978 in O.C. Handa, n. 14, p. 130.

sons, if not having the status of a partner in the polyandrous system of marriage in most cases joined the *saṁgha* (at least some of them). More sons would follow if it were felt that the labour, which the extra pair of hands would contribute to the household, would not be enough to match the productivity on the farm resulting in marginal productivity. The argument has been advanced that the Tibetans were very well aware of the dangers of marginal productivity on the farmland, that is why the sons (mostly younger) were sent to the monastery to act as a check on the reproduction, which otherwise world have serious economic consequences. For leading a celibate and cut off life, the monk was compensated by his own family and the entire villagers who contributed liberally, as we have seen an enormous part of their earnings. In other words, the families were contributing to the *gompa*s for the upkeep of their own brethren that by extension would mean for their own survival. Monk levy was practised in pre-modern Tibet where every family had to send a male and in some cases a female to the *gompa* or *ani-gompa* respectively like the agricultural tax, wherein the tax paying *miser* could substitute someone else for his allotted labour services. The household could also get a substitute in case they could not provide the requisite member of monks/nuns such a levy was called *tra'ahe* in Tibetan, whereas in Ladakh it was the royal dictum that every household send at least one son to the monastery.

Analysis of this variety tend to over emphasise the role of economy while suggesting that the villagers acted purely out of motivation for the reason of avoiding marginal productivity. The character of the Tibetan showed, as we have already seen the three orientations the *bodhi, karma* and pragmatic orientations. For achieving or even attempting to achieve in this direction, the most favoured means in Mahāyāna Buddhism were the rituals, the proper conduct of which would only help in attaining a favourable rebirth, good harvests, negate evil spirits and above all maintain the cosmic universal cycle. Recitation of *mantra*s played a primal role in this process which is why the readings from the *Kangyur* and *Tangyur* and other religious texts were held compulsory. Sending a son to the monastery, therefore, ensured the continuity of the rituals, which is why the 'endowing' of a son to the monastery stood high in the order of merit acquiring acts. Monk levy apart, some percentage of young boys entered the monastery attracted by the philosophy for which they held a deep conviction. Another widespread notion is that monks were recluses totally divorced from the society, which is only a misnomer. We have seen how a large percentage of novices did not don the robes but led a relatively secular life. Monks also went home to help during the harvest. In extreme cases when the son's presence at home was a vital necessity, he left the order and entered secular life after getting the necessary approval from the monastic authorities.[38] Thus, the monastic order had all the necessary sanctions to allow a smooth functioning of socio-religious as well as economic affairs of the society which were all closely interlinked.

Conclusion

Tibetan society followed two forms of production, the agrarian and the pastoral, both nestled in their respective eco-zones. Trade was an emergent field overemphasised by travellers who have generalised on the average Tibetan's aptitude for trade. The government, monasteries and the aristocrats levied taxes on the lands that fell in their respective jurisdictions and also on the cattle they owned. Suffering from paucity of labour, the *tre-ba* farmed the land with the help of the *duchung* who were lower in social and economic status to them. Labour was provided in the form of cultivation and other aspects like transport by the *tre-ba,* which was a part of their tax obligations. Mobility was also noticed among the *tre-ba,* who were the dynamic element in the Tibetan production system.

Buddhist influence permeated on the mind of the average Tibetan in pre-modern Tibet and conditioned his choices. Income was spent on the monasteries in various forms like

38. *The Blue Annals*, p. 95. Gives an early instance of a monk becoming a layman.

gifts, endowments, payment for ritual services, all amounting to around roughly 50 per cent of the post-tax earnings. Aristocrats also borrowed money at interest to 'invest' in this direction, as it was believed to be an investment for a favourable after life, i.e., rebirth. The *labrangs* and monasteries also invested in lands, livestock, trade ventures and money-lending. The surplus of the *gompas* and *labrangs* increased due to the frugal living of the monks and high returns in these ventures. In addition to providing ritual and religious services, their main pre-occupation, they also doubled up as doctors (*amchis*), painters of *thankas* and other services like printing of religious books (the main work at the Narthang monastery). In addition to land, livestock and cash, the living Buddha was also counted as an economic asset both in Tibet and Mongolia, where similar economic patterns existed only with a preponderance of pastoralism. All *gompas* did not participate in the money-lending activities.

Surplus was invested by the *gompas* in conducting festivals and religious services for the betterment of all and more importantly channellised in the direction of building newer and more *gompas*. The ultimate ideal was to ensure more and more monks who would lead to salvation from the cyclic existence of birth and rebirth.

6

Gompa and Polity

TIBETAN polity passed through various stages of evolution finally leading to the establishment of the Dalai Lama's government. Here, we shall see the ascendancy of the *gompa* and increasing monastic input into polity during the main phases, which are early rule of the Yarlung Kings, Śākya Polity and then the rule of the Dalai Lamas. The main focus would be on the historical developments that are traced chronologically and contextually along with their implications for the polity.

Traditional Tibetan historians trace a royal lineage of divine origin claiming the total number of kings are 41 beginning with Nyatri Tsenpo in 127 BC and ending with Langdarma, the forty-first king. Nyatri Tsenpo is credited with unifying the various Tibetan tribes, documents found at Tun-huang in eastern Turkestan recently also testify to this.[1] The basic constituents of a state are a taxing authority, an army and a surplus producing strata above all. For 'surplus' is a very questionable term and the quantum of surplus produced depends on the coercive power of the ruling class. Coercion is always not by military power, ideology playing a great role, for it also serves to legitimise the rule of the surplus appropriating classes. The food producers in Tibet, we have seen were the agriculturists and the nomads, some of the latter have even to this day survived keeping intact to a certain level, tribal forms of socio-political organisation, the

1. R.A. Stein, *Tibetan Civilisation*, tr. J.E. Stapleton Driver, 1972, p. 61.

Goloks and the Hor people being examples. The conditions for a good surplus were all found in the Yarlung valley and it is therefore no wonder that all the kings upto Langdarma had their base here, this lineage also being commonly referred to as the Yarlung kings. Bon was the pre-Buddhist religion of Tibet and the expanding state apparatus needed some cultural elements which are the correlates of an advanced material culture like a script which came to Tibet via India leaving a Buddhist imprint though Thonmi Sambotha who brought the script from India to Tibet was not a monk.

Songtsen Gampo, Trisong Detsen and Ralpachen were fondly remembered by the later kings and nobility, of Tibet for their services to the kingdom. In addition to being great patrons of Buddhism, they were strong monarchs who expanded the kingdom, particularly Songtsen Gampo through his matrimonial alliances with the Chinese and Nepalese that saw the rise of Buddhism in Tibet. There was no doubt that the armies of Tibet were strong enough to cause damage to China[2], who like India were kingdoms practising settled agriculture and constantly in dread of the 'barbarian' pastoralists. China adopted a policy of taming these peoples on the frontiers through a policy of gifts giving termed as tribute and gradually Sinicising them.[3] Tibet was a unified nation during the reign of Songtsen Gampo though not much is known in detail about the administrative system. Such practices of endowing monasteries with land were to provide sustenance for an institution, in this case the *gompa,* which would act as a centralising agent. Langdarma's period brought to fore the ire of Bon ministers who saw in Buddhism a threat to their established position leading to an anarchic situation and earning for Langdarma the label of an 'apostate' who brought bad tidings signifying a dark age. Such accounts portray the fall of the Yarlung dynasty and the consequent anarchy as a 'Dark Age'.

---

2. *The Blue Annals,* pp. 47-52.

3. Warren W. Smith, 'The ideological basis of China's Tibet policy', *Tibetan Review,* vol. 23, no.11, November 1988, pp. 13-14.

In brief, we may see the shifts in polity from pre-Buddhist to Gelugpa rule. The effects of the monastic involvement in polity are enormous for it gave Tibet the distinct shape of polity that was a unique development unparalleled in the human history. We shall first examine the polity of pre-Buddhist Tibet.

Paucity of material makes the writing of the early history of Tibet somewhat problematic as the later versions betray a religious tinge which is apparent when they glorify Songtsen Gampo and vilify Langdarma, the former for his assumed contribution to Buddhism which is presented in a large than life way, and the latter for the destruction of the doctrine. These accounts are the work of lama scholars whose bias is not easy to fathom out. By using Chinese sources we can arrive at a more complete picture particularly the royal annals of the Sung and Sui dynasty which portray Tibet as a military warrior nation where 'men were engaged in military activities'. Those who were strong were made leaders; and the weak were forced to be subjects.[4] Early Tibetan legal system is also portrayed as a system where physical force or the threat of its use was prevalent along with magic in the swearing in of authority. Such practices are reminiscent of the ancient code of Hammurabi which prescribed an eye for an eye and a tooth for a tooth, sounding crude to the civilized 'culture states' of that time unlike the predominant pastoral society where they were practised. Pastoral societies or pre-state societies had a martial spirit often expressed in raids and loot over cattle of the neighbours kingdom. In course of time under dynamic leadership these hordes attacked the neighbouring civilizations, a pattern of conflicts which characterise ancient history, e.g., the Gothic attacks on the Roman Empire, the Hūṇ invasion of Europe and Asia including India. It was during the reign of the so-called religious kings that most of the energies were diverted in this domain, between AD 634 and 849, nineteen instances of major conflicts occurred between China and Tibet of which 90 per cent were Tibetan aggressions against China consisting of large armies of over

4. Dawa Norbu, *Tibet The Road Ahead*, 1997, p. 365.

a million soldiers, the most famous of them being Songtsen Gampos' two million strong army which marched into China demanding the hand of princes Wen Cheng[5] from the Tang Emperor Dai Zung in AD 640. An equally large army captured the Chinese capital (Sian) and installed for a while a Tibetan prince as an Emperor of China. The apogee was reached in AD 783 by the conclusion of a treaty between China and Tibet by which Tibetan military attention was diverted to the west against the Arabs.[6]

The historical context was such that China was a 'culture state' inhabited by peoples practising settled agriculture always in dread of the predatory hordes as her north-west border that was the soft-underbelly and thereby these invading hordes were referred to as barbarians. Such parallels were also found in India when the successive hordes of the Śakas, Pārthians, Pahlavas, Kuṣāṇas and Hūṇas were designated as *mlecchas* or barbarian. These *mlecchas* were co-opted into the Indian polity by ascribing to them the status of fallen kṣatriya whose place in society had gone down because of degenerate practices, but could be gained by performance of the proper rituals whereby they could regain their kṣatriya or royal status complete with a new genealogy and conforming to the cultural patterns prevalent in the Indian areas. In China, they tried to contain these invasions of the barbarians by 'tributes' and matrimonial alliances.[7]

The fall of the centralised Tibetan Empire and the kingless age (*Silbo 'dus)* did not led to any large-scale raids or army organisation. Thereafter monasteries sprang up from Ngari under the patronage of Yeshes Ö till the whole of Tibet was converted to Buddhism except a few Bon enclaves. Martial spirit survived only among the Khampas, the people of Kham in eastern Tibet. Power now passed on to the lamas and being ardent Buddhists they abhorred the use of force. This is not to say that militarism completely disappeared from Tibetan

5. Dawa Norbu, *Tibet The Road Ahead*, p. 367.
6. *Ibid.*
7. Warren W. Smith, n. 4, p. 13.

society. Mongol support was the basis for the Śākyapas rise to power, which would have been unthinkable for the Śākya *paṇḍita* without the backing of the 3,00000 strong force of Godan khan. The turning point was that a strong standing Tibetan army was not developed and even in later period during the Dalai Lamas period, the Dzungar Mongols assured the Gelugpas rise to power. But even they desisted from militarising the society. The reasons for which are clear as also the reason for the failure of kingship to resurface after the second diffusion of Buddhism. Tibet was converted to Buddhism after the Second Diffusion after which the rulers lost the mandate to rule, as sanctioned by their native religion, Bon. Though it took a period of about four hundred years for this whole process to crystallise and the Buddhists also tended to use *Bonpo* notions of kingship by appropriating them. The legitimising authority were the lamas backed by external forces, Yuans in the case of the Śākyapas and the Mongols and later the Manchus in the case, of the Dalai Lamas.

Buddhist revival under the aegis of Yeshe Ö of the Guge kingdom saw a monastery building spree in the western Himālayas. Yeshe Ö presented Rinchen Zangpo with the estate of zer in western Tibet which is another example of a land grant.[8] During the reign of Ralpachen, the practice of endowing monasteries with land was first started.[9] Monasteries became the torchbearers of culture and being endowed with enough material resources in the form of land and property, they soon emerged as centres of scholarship, agents of religious and ideological dissemination, synthesising *Bonpo* and Buddhist elements. The rise of sects was another milestone development in Tibetan political history for it inaugurated a pan-Tibetan network whose institutional base was the monastery. A related development was the obscuring of royal power and its relegation to the background with the rise of sects, though it took some centuries to achieve this. Religion at many points of time took a backseat as Tibet had

8. *The Blue Annals,* p. 68.
9. O.C. Handa, *Buddhist Monasteries in Himachal Pradesh*, 1987, p. 119.

to witness lot of bloodshed caused by internecine tussles among the various sects for reasons largely political. The Nyingmapas (the first) were the first school to flourish on Tibetan soil. Atiśa's visit to central Tibet in AD 1024 and the consequent religious ferment engendered by his visit brought into being most of the new sects, of which was the Kadampa school stressing on austerity and discipline. To mark out the older school, the term Nyingampas was used who were the most 'shamanic' among the sects if we use the terms shamanic and clerical as bipolar opposites. The Śākyapa school founded by Kon Chogyal Pho and some subsects of Kagyupa were popular and began establishing monastic centres with popular and aristocratic support. Particularly, the Śākyapas who became very popular and it was the Śākya Lamas who ruled Tibet for a period of ninety-six years from 1254 to 1350.[10] The rule of the Śākyapas saw the union of Tibet that had been disrupted since the time of Langdarma but at a price, Tibet became intertwined in the central Asian politics and its reflections had bearings on her polity permanently.

Genghiz Khan who styled himself as the scourge of mankind founded an empire comprising China and parts of Central Asia. Tibet warded off the ever present Mongol danger by paying tributes and thus maintaining a smooth working relationship which was however not destined to last forever due to the non-payment of tribute. Danger in the form of Mongol conquest was looming large but by a strange turn of events the erudite and well-respected Śākya *paṇḍita* converted Godan Khan. The latter was so taken away by his spirituality that the old terms of relationship were cast aside and a new patron-priest relationship called *yon-chod* relationship, was established, thus marking a turning point not only in Tibetan but in the whole Central Asian history.[11] The *yon-chod* relationship is a contentious issue in Sino-Tibetan relations with China claiming that it was a tributary

---

10. Hugh. E. Richardson, 'Political Role of the Four Sects in Tibetan History', *Tibetan Review,* vol. 11, no. 9, September, 1976, pp. 18-19.
11. Tsepon W.D. Shakabpa, *Tibet — A Political History,* 1988, pp. 61-4.

relationship and the obverse interpretation applied by the Tibetans who claim it is a purely patron-priest relationship is one of the examples among many such extant relationships in Central Asia. Śākya *paṇḍita* was offered the rule of Tibet to which he agreed and also to make the Śākyapa sect the only legal sect thus outlawing other sects to which he did not agree.[12]

Monasteries were now the centralising agents of the state apparatus as the Śākyapas assumed the rule all over Tibet, now a unified politico-administrative entity due to the Mongol efforts. Bitter feuds broke out amongst monasteries owing allegiance to the Śākyapas and the Kagyupa monastery of Drikung, which controlled several Trikhor (administrative districts) and did not take kindly to Śākyapa hegemony thus contesting it by armed warfare. This bane of armed warring groups was to be a part of Tibet's political spectrum till the Gelugpa consolidation. As already mentioned, the extra-territorial actors, viz., the Mongols and the Chinese had also influenced the political events. The fall of the Mongol Yuan dynasty in China had reverberations in Tibet signalling the end of the Śākyapa rule, making way for the Phagmodrugpa branch of the Kagyupa School who defeated the Śākyapas in an outright battle in 1354.[13] The *trikhor* or administrative divisions held by the opposing Drikhung monastery of the Kagyupas were dissolved and in their place came up *dzongs*. A system of governors who had local revenue jurisdiction overseen by the monastic lord was set-up in all districts. Such a monastic lord, the head of the dynasty started his succession through the nearest male kinsman of the celibate lama. Internal factions which were the bane of the Mongol overlords and their Tibetan allies had caused much damage earlier, resurfaced again with new alliances and counter alliances. So complex was the political chessboard of Tibet that from a history of the monastery of Phenpo Nalendra, we get an example of how the abbots were just pawns in the great power

---

12. Tsepon W.D. Shakabpa, *Tibet — A Political History,* 1988, p. 65.
13. Hugh E. Richardson, n. 7, p. 19.

game, the dynamics of which were beyond their control.[14]

Changchub Gyaltsen, coeval with the decline of the imperial Yuan dynasty, overthrew Chinese influence in dress, mannerisms and customs. The Mings succeeded the Yuans but did not have any allies in Tibet and courted the Black hat Karmapa sect of the Kagyupa who had connections with the late Yuan Emperors. The Mings termed their visits as 'tribute missions'. Yet another contentious term, for the Karmapas never fully controlled Tibet, their main area of operation being Eastern Tibet.[15] Central Tibet was in a state of tension with old rivalry erupting between Ü and Tsang. During this period, the Karmapas were religiously the dominant for over a hundred and a fifty years. Political power was not fully in the hands of the monks as the lay nobles were equally represented as ministers and also as financial backers in the political scenario. The Princes of Gyantse were showing great enthusiasm to fill up the political vacuum caused by the weakening of the Central Government but were overridden by Rimpung, a lay noble of Tsang. The working arrangement was such that the lay nobles who were militarily and administratively the most powerful in Tibet had an alliance with the religious lamas for benefits, obviously for legitimisation. Rimpung was not very much in the good books of the Karmapas, where he does not figure till 1480 after which political expediency brought the Karmapas and the Rimpung leader together in open hostility to the Gelugpas at Lhasa.

Tsongkhapa, a great thinker and a saint founded the Gelugpa sect after early education under the Karmapa and the Bodangpa won the support of the Phagmodurpa Gongma and his local representative Kyishoe, eventually enabling him to found the famous monastery at Ganden in 1409. What

---

14. David P. Jackson, *The Early Abbots of 'PHAN-PO-NALENDRA', The Vicissitudes of a great Tibetan Monastery in the Fifteenth Century,* 1989, p. 20.

15. Wang Jiawei & Nyima Gyaincain, *The Historical Status of China's Tibet*, 1997, pp. 38-9.

led to the fame of Tsongkhapa was his unique personality, his saintliness, purity and sincerity that attracted the enthusiasm of the lay people, nobles and ordinary folk. Lhasa was put on the religious map by Tsongkhapa who established the tradition of the Great Prayer Ceremony, thus, rekindling the importance of the neglected holy city of Lhasa. Ganden became a famous centre in course of time due to the austerities of the monks who founded a new order called Gandenpa, later named Gelugpa after the death of the Master Tsongkhapa. Primacy of the Sūtras over the Tantras and austere life were the cardinal virtues of the Gelugpas who wanted to be exemplary thus winning over the laity by moral persuasion.[16] With the growth of Lhasa as a religious centre it attracted the Karmapas thereby creating new political alignments in the form of allying with Donyod Dorje, the Rimpung leader and the Karmapas. Donyod Dorje laid seize to Lhasa from 1498 to 1517 creating hard times for the Gelugpas who were removed from the Great Prayer Festival. Religious boundaries were being redrawn with Gelugpas being persecuted and not other sects like the Nyingmapa, Śākyapa, Naropa and Jonangpa. In the same manner in which the Rimpung came to power by pulling the carpet under the feet of the Phagmodrugpa, in about 1575, Tsheten Dorje a minister of the Rimpungpa rose to power steadily and patronised the Karmapas.

Events till 1617 had been primarily militaristic depending on the swinging fortunes of the Gelugpas and Karmapas and their patrons resulting in armed struggles in which even monks participated. Noteworthy is the struggle between the Karmapa and the Rimpungpa allied on one side versus the monks of Drepung and Sera at the other end for the control of Lhasa. For a time it seemed that Gelugpa fortunes were in the wane with Yonten Gyatso the second Dalai Lama who was also the great grandson of Altan Khan found his main strength, the Mongol horsemen expelled. The Gelugpa's main patrons the Tumed Mongols who comprised the fighting force

---

16. Ram Rahul, *The Dalai Lama The Institution*, 1985, p. 4.

found their influence and fortune wilting in their home country. And in Tibet it was so serious that the news about the new reincarnation of the Dalai Lama, Ngawang Lobsang Gyatso was kept a secret obviously out of fear of the Karmapas.[17] Gelugpa fortunes turned on to a new upswing with Gushri Khan the leader of Qoshot tribe of the Oriats becoming their new patron. In his zeal and new enthusiasm matched by his energy and dynamism an all out offensive was counted against the Karmapas who allied with Chagtu the leader of the Khalka Mongols who was killed by Gushri Khans' troops. Gelugpa's finally gained an upper hand in the conflict which spread all over the Tibetan culture area except Lahaul which escaped on account of it isolation.[18]

Gelugpa consolidation that started under the able governorship of the great fifth Dalai Lama, Sonam Gyatso and Gushri Khan, saw the administration being refurbished and thoroughly overhauled. All of Tibet came under Gelugpa rule but for the large estates such as Śākya and other[19] enclaves as Lhagyari. Monasteries were carefully restored while a good number of Karmapa monasteries were converted to Gelugpa, all headed by abbots handpicked and loyal. It goes to the credit of Gushri Khan's generosity and sacrifice of political ambition to make the Gelugpa consolidation possible.

The system of government started by the Fifth Dalai Lama in the seventeenth century remained in force till the Chinese takeover (or peaceful liberation of Tibet). Suffice it to say that it continued till the full pre-modern period. Various terms have been used to describe the government ranging from a feudal kingdom to bureaucracy,[20] and we shall examine the system and working of the government. First, the government headed by the Dalai Lama itself was a 'religious institution',

17. Hugh E. Richardson, n. 7, p. 21.

18. O.C. Handa, n. 5, p. 69.

19. C.W. Casinelli and Robert B. Ekvall, *A Tibetan Principality. The Political System of Saskya*, 1969, p. 214.

20. Franz Michael, *Rule by Incarnation: Tibetan Buddhism and its role in society and state,* 1982, p. 24.

but the Dalai Lama as a religious leader was also the temporal head of all Tibet. The term used by the Tibetan State to call their government was *Bio-zhung-cho-sid-nyi-dan* which literally means a blend of religion and politics. Ecclesiastical officers did not head all departments nor were all sections wholly religious. At the apex of the socio-political system was the Dalai Lama, the ruler of Tibet whose authority was unchallenged, save except during his minority when a regent could exercise the right on behalf of the Dalai Lama. Many Dalai Lamas passed away at young ages during which time the administration was carried out on their behalf by the regents. For a good, number of years, the regents governed Tibet but it lacked the effectiveness of the Dalai Lama's rule because the regent, usually a high lama had his independence curtailed by the committee which could remove him thereby diluting his powers greatly.[21] Secondly, it led to ineffective and indecisive periods in Tibetan history thus seriously affecting the socio-political system. All this was due to the absence of charisma that was part of the Dalai Lama's personality, the same charisma missing from the regents. The 'Regent' (Tib. *Desi*) was chosen by the Tsongdu from among the *tulku*s of the four monasteries near Lhasa (known as big monasteries). The Regent had become so powerful that from 1757 to 1895, the Regents held the real power as many Dalai Lamas passed away before their majority. From 1751 to 1850 the regents ruled for 77 per cent of the time.

We shall examine the structure of the Dalai Lamas' government, modes of recruitment and functioning. There were two divisions the secular and religious establishment, the latter was handled by the *Tseyigtsang* (the peak ecclesiastical secretariat). At the head of the ecclesiastical secretariat were four grand secretaries (*Drungyig Chemo*), who had the powers to deal with all the affairs of the monasteries ranging from disputes, subsidies and any other problem like monastic finances, disputes between a monastery and laity. Around a million of the Tibetan population were

21. Ram Rahul, *The Government and Politics of Tibet*, 1971, p. 23.

monks and the power of the monasteries was religiously, economically and politically a potent force. So dealing with such, a strong element of the Tibetan polity was a great test as it could determine the future course of the country and it is no wonder that the four grand secretaries were called the four inner pillars[22] (*rangi Kawazhi*).

This institution had its origin during the period of the Dalai Lama VII. Powers of the *Yiktsang* were not incumbent on all the monks of Tibet as the three monasteries of Lhasa, Sera, Drepung and Ganden were excluded from its jurisdiction as these three monasteries administered themselves. Functioning from Potala, the *Yiktsang* was also referred to as *Tse Yiktsang. Tse* meant peak obviously referring to the Potala. Entry to this monastic service was a much-coveted desire among ordinary Tibetans as it pro-vided upward mobility, monetary power and satisfaction. The training for the boys at the *Tsebatan* (the peak school) was around fourteen to twenty years with a stay of around three to four years and after this period they were absorbed into the government service on passing the requisite exams and above all on their relations with the *Drungyig Chemos* whose say mattered. *Gegen Chemo* was the title of the principal to whom applications were addressed for admission in this prestigious school, whose normal intake was at the most thirty boys, most of who were relations of monks, former monk officials and noble families. *Tsedrung* was the name of the monk officials of the government whose rank was exactly the same as the *Shadrung* in the secular wing of the government. Details of all the monk cadre officials were listed in a register called *Tsen Shung* and maintained in the office of the *Yiktsang* from which the list the potential officials were selected. An interesting observation about the monk officials is that among the three or four hundred of them at least two-thirds of them were nominated for reason of practical difficulties in keeping the 253 rules prescribed in the *Vinaya* and also indicative of the preference for administrative

---

22. Ram Rahul, *The Government and Politics of Tibet*, 1971, pp. 15-16.

service. In pre-modern Tibet, the role of the government was limited, the ratio of the officials to the population standing at around one official of every four to six thousand people, the total number of officials being seven hundred or so[23] for a population of three million. The headmen and elders, in their nomadic camps adjudicated disputes in the villages by the leaders. Famous monks were also called on to settle disputes among the lay people on account of the respect they had for the monks. Moral superiority was what distinguished the monk officials from the secular officials even though the official rank of both of them was the same. Monk officials gave the Tibetan state and society the value system of after life (the *bodhi* orientations of which they were the examples). Secular administration was not composed fully of lay people even though they dominated, as some monk officials were there too. The office of the Prime minister (*silon*) and the cabinet were the important pillars of the secular administration. The thirteenth Dalai Lama appointed three prime ministers, of which two were laymen and one was a monk while the fourteenth Dalai Lama appointed two prime ministers, one monk and one layman thus showing that the secular administration was also staffed by monk officials. The *Kashag Lhengye* was the council of ministers which was staffed by four ministers (*kalon*), three lay officials and one monk was called the *Chihikawashi* (four outside pillars) in local parlance.[24]

Appointment to the *Kashag* was made by the Dalai Lama or by the regent during the Dalai Lamas infancy and it was a time honoured convention that the Dalai Lama never appointed any of his relatives to any important post as it would amount to concentration of political authority giving rise to larger questions. A departure from this practice was made when the thirteenth Dalai Lama appointed his cousin as the prime minister. In their day-to-day functions, the *Kashag* was assisted by the *Kadrung* (secretaries of the

---

23. Geoffrey Samuel, n. 1, pp. 25-31.
24. Ram Rahul, n. 20, p. 25.

Kashag), lay officials of the *Kashag* who dealt with the correspondence of the *Kashag* and below them the secretaries called *Shapa* (*kashag* Clerks). Powers and responsibilities of the *Kashag* were immense concerning landholdings, taxes, and new rates of taxes, special exemptions for taxes, revenue, expenditure. It was also the highest court of appeal for lay Tibetans all over the country delivering appellate jurisdiction from civil and military officials like the *Dapon* (arrow chief, a sort of colonel), the *Dzongpon* (District Governor) and the *Mipon* (City Magistrate). For cases relating to the members of a *Depon* family (descendants of the early kings of Tibet) on any such serious case the *Kashag* had original jurisdiction. Only the Dalai Lama could over rule the *Kashag's* verdict but unlike modern day cabinets, the *Kashag's* power was seriously limited, as it had to share power with the *Tsongdu.* In respect of the political matters and the monkhood as a whole could only be tried by the *Yiktsang,* however important or serious the case may be.

Important departments were the *Tsikhang* or Finance department, *Tsongdu* or assembly that need to be discussed in detail to see the whole Tibetan polity. Of the secular wings, the *Tsikhang* was an important part of the state, created during the reign of the seventh Dalai Lama, it was presided over by four lay officials of the fourth rank (originally three till the eighteenth century) known as *Tsipon*s. (Comptrollers of finance) who were below the *Kashag.* All the four comptrollers had three or four junior accountants of the sixth grade, all belonging to the lay rank. Recruitment to the *Tsikhang* was much like the *Yiktsang.* The ages of the recruits were around fourteen to twenty with the training period going for three to four years. One of the important duties of the *Tsipon*s was to conduct meetings of both the *Tsongdu Dupa* (small assembly) and the *Tsongdu Gyezom* (Great Assembly). Their role was of an administrative nature towards the procedural side verifying whether all the people in the attendance list were present, and deciding with the *Drungyig Chemos* whether any agreement had been reached in any matter under discussion.

In Tibet, the Assembly was called the *Tsongdu,* an institution of antiquity, which took over the functions of the great monasteries and lay representatives of Sera, Ganden and Drepung as they were the ones who conducted official business with India, China and Nepal. *Tsongdu Dupa* (small assembly) and *Tsongdu DimBu / Gyezom* (great assembly) were the two kinds of assemblies. Differences between them were only minor in terms of composition and functions. The *Tsongdu Dupa* was made up of the *Drungyig Chemo*s, the *Tsipon*s, the *Dapon*s and all other officials of the fourth rank besides two officials of the fifth rank. Two or three sons of nobles attended by rotation besides aristocrats. There was no fixed agenda for the *Tsongdu Dupa* that was summoned by the *Kashag* on a notification (*dato*) but without spelling the agenda. Meetings took place in the *Chuglhagkhang* of the Potala Palace and the outcome of these discussions were of an advisory nature which was not binding on the *Kashag* and if any matter was of great consequence then the *Tsongdu Dimbu* would deliberate upon it.

The *Tsongdu Dimbu* had a more broad-based composition representing all sections of the society of every class. All lay and monk officers with the exceptions of the *Kalon*s and the *Chikyab Khenpo* attended its meetings. The *Khenpo*'s of Sera, Drepung and Ganden along with nine representatives (*thumi*s) of the three great monasteries along with representatives of every class and occupation artisans, boatmen, soldiers and tradesmen and the members of the *Tsongdu Dupa* participated in the discussions.[25] The agenda for the *Tsongdu Dimbu* was not known till the start of the meeting when the *Kashag* communicated it. Thereafter the members of this House finally arriving at a conclusion debated it upon. The *Drungyig Chemos*, the *Tsipon*s and the presiding officers would then communicate this resolution of this assembly to the *Kashag* which would them submit it to the Dalai Lama along with its opinion. The opinion of the *Kashag* could be disregarded by the Dalai Lama but not that of the

25. Ram Rahul, p. 3.

Tsongdu Dimbu which acted as a check on the Dalai Lama's power. Relations of Tibet with China, India, Nepal had to necessarily go through the *Tsongdu Dimbu* and instances are there to show how it took tough decisions.

Treasuries were of two kinds, the *Labrang Chagzo* located in the *Chuglhakhang* the main treasury of the Government established during the reign of the fifth Dalai Lama VIII. Here also the monastic official was one among the three, the other two belonging to the *Tsedrung* cadre and held the fourth rank.[26] Receipts of revenue came from a narrow tax base as monasteries were exempted from taxation. Gold from the gold mines of Kham and Ngari along with turquoises and coral formed part of the receipts. Loans to persons and remission of revenue were the other routine jobs taken up by the treasury. There were two other treasuries, the Reserve treasury (*Namse Ganzo*) (Treasury of the Son of the god of Wealth) and the Dalai Lama's Private Treasury. The Reserve treasury was stocked immensely with gold, silver and precious stones to be used only in times of national emergency. In contrast the Dalai Lama's own treasury whose main income was from the offerings of the pilgrims, income from his personal estates (*Labrang*) and a part of the gold mined at Ngari was expended for buying his personal items and making presents. The Chief Treasurer of the Dalai Lama acted as the director of the miracle and mystery plays performed throughout the country by actor minstrels belonging to different troupes to inoculate among people the deep great significance of the important episodes of Tibetan history. *Pho Kang* was the army treasury and independent of the other treasuries but not of much consequences as militarisation was given a low priority the Lamaist government.[27] Celebrated monasteries such as the Ramoche monastery, Samye, Tibet's first monastery had their own treasuries free from government control and managed entirely by the monasteries themselves which is a pointer to the vast

26. Ram Rahul, p. 33.

27. *Ibid.*, p. 35.

financial control of the monasteries, thus narrowing the scope of the government in a crucial area.

It has been conveyed by a majority of Tibetologists that the government at Lhasa was the government controlling all of Tibet, which leads us to the assumption that the huge monastic element in Lhasan polity was replicated everywhere and other systems of political organisation were absent. To some extent it is true that the Central Government at Lhasa had wide powers but examples of 'autonomous' political units like Saskya, nomadic areas, enclaves in Kham go to point out that there were different arrangements and institutions for it has been the subject of a well documented study by Casinelli and Ekvall[28] and their study shows that though the power of the *HKrichen* was not absolute he held vast powers like revenue collection and enforcing monk levy both of which were crucial to the politico-economic structure for the ideal of Saskya as well as of all Tibet was to support more and more monks for the betterment of state and society.[29] Saskya assumes importance for another reason that is was situated in the centralised agricultural zone having a high number (around 104), of *gompas* and yet had a different political system. The hereditary ruler of Saskya was the *HKrichen* whose origins go back to the thirteenth century when a Phags Pa gave noble status to his military and civil officials including headmen. Thus, the Saskya polity represents the best example of an autonomous polity.

Tibetan polity is based on the dichotomy of the ecclesiastical and the secular class in the administrative structure (*Tse-drungs* and *Sho-drungs*) who should theoretically have had representation in a fifty-fifty ratio which was how ever not the case as far as practice was concerned. In reality, the *Tse-drungs* held around 60 per cent of the posts, a good number and they were very crucial because they held important offices.[30] The material elements according to, Bina

28. C.W. Casinelli, no. 18, p. 303.

29. Bina Roy Burman, *Religion and Politics in Tibet,* 1979 p. 55.

30. *Ibid.*, p. 55.

Roy Burman, included the increased state support to monasteries, preserving the social order so as to ensure continuance of the vast monastic assets. Non-material interests included preservation of the conservative thinking inhibiting change, as it would trigger forces detrimental to their faith and indirectly affect their position.

It may be seen that in addition to the monastic element, the aristocratic element was also present in a good percentage among the higher level of officials and the middle level of officials. In fact, the duty of the aristocratic class was to supply officials far the state. Speaking of material interests, both the aristocrat and the monasteries had large estates, which was their economic base. The strengths and merit in the polity were that it attracted new adherents who felt that they could get a place if they had a belief in the system. Moreover monasticism was a very practical mode of social mobility for the vast majority of Tibetans.[31] For example, an ordinary Tibetan from any part of the Tibetan cultural area could rise to one of the exalted positions in the great monasteries of Lhasa due to his erudition and as we have seen a 'Rinpoche' could even start a line of reincarnate lamas or *tulkus*.[32] From a background of the Dalai Lamas we get varied examples of family backgrounds and regions with the second Dalai Lama coming from a Mongolian royal family to the sixth Dalai Lama who came from the Tawang monastery situated at the south-eastern most end of the Tibetan cultural area. Probably the fact that ordinary people could rise to exalted positions and also since every family had at least one member in the *gompa* that we have seen was due to marginal productivity. Some monasteries like the south monastery at Saskya did nct lend money and enforced rules fond in the *Vinaya,* strictly and thus attracted popular respectability.[33]

31. Sherpa Tulku, Khamlung Tulku, Alexander Berzin and Jonathan Landaw, 'The structrue of the Gelug Monastic Order', *The Tibet Journal,* vol. 2, no. 3, Autumn 1977, pp. 67-9.

32. *Ibid.*

33. C.W. Casinelli, n. 18, p.

Reincarnation was a great political innovation for it helped to prevent familial and other forms of rivalry and at the same time allowing the whole political process to continue undisturbed. Originally an innovation of the Karmapas, all sects including Bon have adopted this practice which attained its greatness among the Gelugpas. The first reincarnation of Gendun Durub was recognised in the personage of Sonam Gyatso, who true to his reputation as the reincarnation of the Grand Lama scaled remarkable heights spreading his name far and wide. Altan Khan a leader of the Tumed Mongols invited Sonam Gyatso in 1577 which led to another patron priest relationship being established, Sonam Gyatso being awarded the title of the Dalai Lama[34] and Altan Khan was reciprocated with the title of *chos-kyi gyal po* (Skt. *dharmarāja*). Relations of such a nature were mutually beneficial inasmuch they legitimised the rule of the patrons. In this case that of Altan Khan who along with his Tumed tribe and a host of allied tribes converted to the Gelugpa sect therefore it was natural that he be recognised as the rightful righteous ruler by none other than the religious head of that sect. For the Gelugpas, the title of Dalai Lama (Wisdom of the Ocean) served to give the royal power behind them, increasing the charisma of the post. Since both the patron and priest had diverse interests, there would never arise the problem of conflict at least immediately in the near future.

A *Tulku* (*sprul Ku*) is a *bodhisattava*, an integral concept in Mahāyāna Buddhism; the Buddha delays his enlightenment repeatedly for the benefit of the whole mankind taking countless births and rebirths in this process. Buddha in the Mahāyāna tradition is a 'saviour', a role having much more social scope than the earlier Buddha of the Hīnayāna tradition wherein he was portrayed as a teacher. In the Tibetan tradition, the living Buddha as the *tulku*s were known performed a wide variety of functions, of particular relevance to our study are the political functions performed by the *tulku*s. There were more than ten thousand *tulku*s in

34. Tsepon W.D. Shakabpa, n. 8, p. 95.

old Tibet performing a wide array of functions as monastic heads, heads of sects, subsects, of monastic complexes and in the person of the Dalai Lama of the Central Government of Tibet itself.

The institution of the *tulku* originates from the concept of the *bodhisattava* who embodies the two distinct qualities of selfless compassion for others (*karma*) and development of wisdom (*prajñā).* Buddha was the first *bodhisattava* and all *bodhisattava*s were to model themselves on the Buddha's actions. Of particular importance to the Mahāyāna Buddhists was the concept of the *pāramitā*s (perfections), references to which abound in Mahāyāna literature. Further the *bodhisattava* faces a dilemma at a point of time later on, whether to use his knowledge for his enlightenment or for the benefit of the larger society and it was not possible to serve diverse interests and then the duty towards the society took precedence which required an altruistic spirit occurring naturally and effortlessly that it was fully internalised in the personalities.[35] In Buddhist tradition, any act *per se* is not taken into account if the larger questions of the totality are not included, e.g., meat-eating is either sinful or permitted depending on the context and motivation. Likewise meditation is at the heart of the *bodhisattava*'s path mentioned in the Mahāyāna texts but the motivation for meditation should not be for one's development only, but increasing ones ability to help others, compassion is an ideal second only to meditation expounded in clear terms in the *Dacabhumika Sūtra* according to which compassion should begin from the practice of generosity and in that *bhūmi* the *bodhisattava* is depicted perfecting the *pāramitā* of generosity and as he goes on through the *bhūmi*s he needs to acquire various forms of knowledge and ability and therefore he seeks proficiency in other systems of knowledge as mastering the Buddhist Sūtras, writing, psychology and so on. Thus, the ideal *bodhisattava* of the early Mahāyānists was a master

---

35. Reginald A. Ray, 'Some Aspects of the *Tulku* Tradition in Tibet', *The Tibet Journal,* 1986, vol. XI, no. 4, Winter 1986, pp. 38-43.

well versed in meditation and knowledge.[36] Contrasted to this developed the ideal of the *siddha* in the Vajrayāna tradition wherein an emphasis was placed on skillful means (*upāya*). Here the *siddha* was a non-erudite householder or wandering *yogī* from the lower castes, and possessing the full range of magical powers and miracles described in the *bhūmi* literature all these are the qualities needed to help others. A synthesis of this *siddha* exemplifying the ideal of the upper *bhūmi bodhisattava* in the direction of reality and immediacy showing a hierarchy of *tulku*s with higher *bodhisattava* at the top, the Dalai Lama being the topmost.[37]

Significant for the polity was the idea of divine kingship, a concept having immense bearings for the polity of Tibet, according to which the ideal *tulku,* i.e., the higher *tulku*s are conceived of a enlightened beings appropriate for the holding of both social and political power to benefit everybody. The symbolism of Buddha Śākyamuni who was predicted to either become a universal sovereign or world renouncer led to the development of a rich hagiography of the *cakravartin* concept of spiritual kingship. In Tibet, the rise of monasteries and later the rise of the *tulku* institution provided a concrete basis for the fusion of religion and politics.

Tibetan monasticism is traced from its beginnings at Samye, in the second half of eighth century AD, but the real spread of monasticism was during the post-Langdarma period, i.e., during the second diffusion when monasteries arose with landed property obviously for their sustenance. An abbot managed these as we presuppose the existence of an organisation, the abbot also had the authority over a province or a smaller geographical area in this age of power vacuum. This period of Tibetan history is a grey area without much research being done but it is possible to delineate certain strands that later seem to coalesce particularly in the case of the development of the *tulku* ideal. Firstly, the difference

---

36. Edward Conze, 'The six Perfections', in Edward Conze, ed., *Buddhist Texts Through The Ages,* 1954, pp. 135-8.

37. Reginald, A. Ray, n. 33, p. 42.

between the *bodhisattava* ideal of India who reincarnates does not give any indication of the date of the specific events of his reincarnation.[38] Such a need was felt in Tibet due to the rise of the great monastic centres started by each sect as the Śākya monastery founded by Kon Chogyal Pho of the Khon family in 1073, the Kagyupa monastery of Dentasil founded by Lama Phagmotru (1110-70) and the Kagyupa centre of Tsurpu founded by Tusum Kyenpa in 1185 who was later to become the first Karmapa heralding the actual process of the *tulku*. All these centres founded during the second spreading of Buddhism had rich local patrons whose munificence led to the development of these centres and their flowering. Abbatial succession followed the family lineage from uncle to nephew. Both advantages and disadvantages were inherent in this system, the advantages being continued monetary and political support of the patron which in the long course of time were, weighed by the disadvantages. These were in the form of monastic involvement in sectarian politics in the form of clan rivalries often being bloody and thus negating the Buddhist ethic of non-violence.[39] It also embroiled the abbots in the political arena so that they were viewed as representatives of the patrons family which must have lent a considerable blow to the 'Charisma' coming in the way of the cross class unification of the allegiance holders of that monastery. Nyingmapa tradition occasionally talks of treasure hunters of the *terma literature* (*tertons*) who take rebirth at intervals, identifying with his predecessor to continue the *bodhisattava* activity.[40] Turning to the Karmapa, we find the first reincarnation in the being of Chadzin (later the second Karmapa, Karma Pakshi (1206-83). Reginald A. Ray has outlined the context mentioned above and also the reason for the rise of the reincarnations, first among the Karmapa sect. According to him the Karmapas had a diverse body of patrons instead of a single patron. So there was no single

38. Reginald A. Ray, pp. 44-7.
39. *Ibid.*
40. *Ibid.*, pp. 44-7.

dominant family insisting on the control and succession.[41] Another contributing factor must have been the insistence of the Karmapa's on relative financial independence as a necessary precondition for the maintenance of the vitality of one's spiritual lineage and teachings, a practice prevalent among the Indian *siddha*s who left the monastery to find their burn support and in Tibet in the case of Marpa, it was the financially independent householder. The rules for the reincarnation of a lama and his time period may have came up due to practical considerations of which the need to fill up the post of abbot within a few years (ordinarily two to three years) may have necessitated the practice of finding a reincarnation by indications in a couple of years. The process of locating a reincarnation was also a creative development on the part of the monastery, which utilised the prevalent traditions of divination in Tibetan society as they appealed to popular taste. The development and incorporation of oracles is also a pointer in this direction. The *gompa* and the *tulku* were integral parts of the Tibetan polity whose functions often mirrored and complemented each others. The main functions of the *gompa* and *tulku* were that they acted as the unifiers, i.e., the centralising authority in the Tibetan society that was characterised by a high degree of decentralisation. Though the Lhasa government at the centre had appointed governors of the provinces, their role was nominal with the power and decision-making only at the local level in the hands of the village and the clan, with the role of the state being limited to tax collection.[42] *Gompa*s and *tulku*s as owners of economic institutions (*labrang*s) performed multifarious functions of an economic nature which lent a semblance of authority and control at the local level. Being the central Buddhist ideal, the *tulku* had a status legitimised by religion and culture, being universally revered by the monasteries, notwithstanding the sectarian difference as each tradition accepted the legitimate status of the other traditions

41. Reginald A. Ray,
42. *Ibid.*, p. 63.

thus bypassing local and regional difference.[43] The *gompas* were replicas of each other all over Tibet following a unified 'Great tradition' in religion and cultural practices in contrast to the local cultures of the diverse regions separated by vast distances. Thus, they were the foci of integration of the political system. *Tulkus* also assumed direct political responsibility of governing the province in many cases. The limitations of the Lhasa government were filled up in many areas by the *tulkus*, particularly in the arena of disputes when the contending parties would listen to the moralising influence of the *tulku*.[44]

As we have seen that monasteries rose to power from AD 1650, in a supreme position with the rise of the fifth Dalai Lama. The three monasteries of Sera, Ganden and Drepung with their large monastic populations as also other big monasteries proved difficult to control and at times they broke out in rebellions. This was due to the fact that big monasteries had a good number of monks called *dob-dob* (literally monastic police) whose duty was policing, particularly evident during the *Monlam Chenmo* festival when the monks of Drepung held power and acted as magistrates in Lhasa. Tengyeling monastery fought openly for the Chinese in 1910. The Dalai Lama's rule was different from that of the previous lama rulers as it provided for the institutionalisation of Charisma (*G-sod-nams dbong-thong* or *Gyinrlahs*). Lamaist ideas on polity directed the use of surplus for the founding of new monasteries, upkeep of the old ones and for other purposes other than militarisation.[45] Thus, a sea change was brought about in the Tibetan polity and policy, i.e., the elimination of the use of force in line with evolving a model of Tibetan polity on the principles of Buddhism, the cardinal point of which was *ahiṁsā* or non-violence.

---

43. Charles Bell, n. 29, p. 171.
44. Ram Rahul, n. 20, pp. 15-16.
45. Hugh Richardson, *Ceremonies of the Lhasa Year,* ed. Michael Aris, 1993, p. 22.

Conclusion

Tibetan society evolved from the union of non-Chinese Chiang tribes and came to the notice of historians when they were unified under the leadership of the Yarlung kings. The armies of the Yarlung kings were a terror in Central Asia, feared for their predatory raids and strong arm tactics forcing the Chinese and Nepalese kings to give their daughters in marriage. The post-Langdarma period saw the fall of the unified state and polity with fragmented political units involved in a hegemonic contestation for power. The monasteries were a new element in these power struggles which charecterised the whole of the period from the eleventh to the sixteenth centuries. Royal and monastic patrons needed each other for benefits of financial and military backing and legitimisation of rule. Sectarian politics and rivalry reached a height during the thirteenth and four-teenth centuries. Monastic involvement in polity brought power to the Śākyapas and the Kagyupas and later to the Gelugpas, all backed by extraterritorial actors, the various Mongol tribes. Two processes started to evolve, one the abolishing of an army in consonance with Buddhist ideas on polity which led to serious consequences for Tibet, the killing of martial spirit and the dependence on external powers. Secondly, the theory of reincarnation served as an innovation to suit the needs of the times of the polity resulting in the institutionalisation of charisma in the person of the reincarnate lama originally started by the Kagyupas, this was taken to its logical extremes by the Gelugpas with the establishment of the office of the Dalai Lama. The final picture emerging in the development of polity in Tibet was the elimination of force as a matter of policy to settle political disputes.

Conclusion

So far there has been a lot of studies on Buddhist ideas, values and precepts but many areas of enquiry like how these ideas have survived through the ages and the organisational bases has not been much explored. This study on the *gompa* has emphasised on the organisational aspect and its multifaceted functional role, which sustained the *gompa* through the centuries. The *gompa* as an organisation came into existence in the seventh century AD with a specific purpose, i.e., to co-ordinate the activities of the Buddhists in the hope of achieving certain specific objectives like the spreading of the *dharma,* salvation to all, reordering the socio-economic and politico-religious life on the basis of Buddhistic principles.

The *mahāvihāra*s of India provided the organisational framework for the *gompa*s which was suitably modified in Tibet keeping in mind the local specificites, thus leading to a typological difference in the monastic organisation during the period called the second diffusion of Buddhism when monasticism really took off. Large monasteries dealing with specialised functions like education, medicine, art, politics and above all management of the economy, which was the base, necessitated formal organisations and subgroups within the *gompa* to perform these specialised functions. Thus, collectivities of inmates within the *gompa*s were formally grouped according to procedures taken from the *Vinaya* and hierarchy of officials was created to render ritual services and other services. This was one of the important reasons for the laity to patronise the *gompa.* Earlier studies have neglected these points as their area of concentration was on the textual literature which did not take into account the contextual realities leading to such mistaken conclusions that the Tibetans were a people obsessed with mysticism.

In the political sphere the main achievements of the *gompa* were the reordering of the polity on the Buddhistic principles of *ahiṁsā* which led to the elimination of use of force as a matter of policy in political struggles. Another contribution was the theory of reincarnation, which drew upon the value orientations of the reformatory movements investing in the person of the *tulku* a charismatic authority. Separated by vast distances and away from the control of Lhasa, vast areas of Tibet were integrated socially and culturally by the *gompa* which consciously perpetuated the 'Great Tradition' in art, literature and religion providing a pan-Tibetan culture area network. It can, thus, be summarised that the *gompa* and the entire Tibetan society should not be seen from a textual point of view but on the basis of the typology of organisational structures. From this we come to know that the average Tibetan was not a mystic but was this worldly.

The Tibetan context thus shows a major departure from its Indian prototype, the *vihāra*. The culmination of this process was the growth of large monasteries, which were called monastic towns like Sera, Ganden, Drepung and Tashilhunpo with vast wealth and landholdings. The wide economic base provided the solid foundations on which the institutional superstructure rested. The economic base was widened continuously by investment in new ventures like trade and largely in land and other miscellaneous services like sale of *thanka*s, *Kangyur* and *Tangyur*, etc., leading to more surplus. The frugal life of the monks and nuns also contributed in this direction to increased surplus.

The surplus was put to use in the founding of new *gompa*s, maintenance of the ritual services and above all the essential services like education and health. In pre-modern Tibet the role of the state was very limited and it was not a welfare state. So it was only logical that an institution like the *gompa* would do this work. This led to a great degree of economic and cultural exchange with the local populace, who were constantly in need of educational, medicinal and other this worldly aids apart from ritual services. This was a main reason for patronising such a large organisation, the *gompa*. Similarly, the *gompa*'s multi-faceted role led to its perpetuation. In contrast to the Theravāda societies where we find forest monks who are total recluses from the society, in Tibet the majority of the people had pragmatic orientations and since the *gompa* served as a rational instrument to implement these pragmatic day-to-day life needs and also as an instrument to implement what the Buddhist ideal prescribed. It became a major institution, occupying a central role in the socio-religious and politico-economic life of Tibet throughout the major part of Tibet's history.

Thus, the main focus of this thesis is how Buddhism survived in Tibet over the centuries in spite of poor material conditions and a difficult terrain. And how did it get so embedded in Tibetan society leading to its perpetuation? Among the findings one main indicator is that the *gompa* performed multifarious functions catering to all types of needs. In the *gompa* the theory of Buddhism was institutionalised so that it could transcend time and space. Therefore, the continuity of Buddhism was due to the multifaceted role of the *gompa*.

Further, the *gompa* should not be seen just as a religious institution, for it performed many socio-cultural and politico-economic functions and in the absence of any other institution of the State, it was the *gompa* that emerged as the superordinate institution.

Elimination of an army and force as a dominant factor in polity along with eliminating famine from Tibet were due to the institutional mediation of the *gompa*.

Glossary

ācārya: preceptor, referred here in the *mahāvihāra*s.

ahiṁsā: non-injury to all sentient beings.

amchi: doctors, in Tibet.

ami: nun in the Tibetan Buddhist tradition.

avatāra: incarnation of a god, here successive incarnations in the Buddhist pantheon, originally a Hindu concept.

bhikku: Pāli word for Sanskrit *bhikṣu*, meaning beggar, the original name given to the Buddha's followers who begged for food.

bodhisattva — literally *bodhi* means enlightenment and *sattva* means essence. A previous incarnation of Buddha who deliberately postpones his enlightenment to work for the betterment of all sentient beings.

Bon: Pre-Buddhist religion of Tibet.

brahmacārin: a student of the Vedas, compulsorily an unmarried boy.

brāhmaṇa: a member of the hereditary priestly caste.

cakra: literally wheel. It is believed in the Hindu/Buddhist world that there are seven major *cakra*s or life-wheels in the body.

Cho-gyal: title of the ruler, literally *dharmarāja*.

Duchung: a section of the misers, lower than the tre'ba.

karma: literally action. *Karma* theory specifies that all sufferings are due to past action in this or earlier lives.

lokapālas: The guardian gods of the universe.

lotsba: translator monks.

maṇḍala: idealised concept of a universe with a sacred centre. Applied in war, architecture, etc.

mantra: ritual chanting of a magical formula that is believed to be sacred and powerful.

Miser: name for farmer in Tibet.

Mt'on gral: liberation through sight.

navatāla: nine spans, in Sanskrit, the measure used to portray gods.

Ngagpa: wandering monks in Tibet.

paṇḍitas: learned men, philosophers.

parivarjaka: wandering ascetic.

paticca-Samuppāda: Chain of dependent originations showing 12 links or causes that leads one from ignorance to suffering.

pīpal: Name of a tree usually associated with seers. Botanical name *ficus religiosa*.

prajñāpāramitā(s): ten perfections of the *bodhisattvas*, name of Buddhist goddess in the Mahāyāna pantheon.

pūjā: a form of worship, now the dominant form among Hindus where symbolic offerings are made to the diety in lieu of animals.

Sārttavāhas: Caravans, mentioned in early Buddhist literature.

Tantra: esoteric religious practices that were part of religion and appropriated in Hindus and Buddhists religions from 6th century AD onwards.

Tre'ba: a section of the misers who paid tax and farmed the land. They were also socially high.

Upaniṣads: mystical texts of the Hindus.

Vinaya Piṭaka: Buddhist canonical text that specifies rules relating to the organisation of the *saṁgha*.

Vipaśyana: A system of meditation that leads to the stilling of the mind.

Yidam: Tibetan word for tutelary deities, believed to posess great power.

Appendix I

Early Indian and Tibetan Monasteries

Nālandā: Nālandā *mahāvihāra* was founded by Śakrāditya during the Gupta times and developed into a monastic university, which functioned from AD 450 to 1100. As a centre of study its fame lay in its different 'School of Studies' attracting students and scholars from far and wide like Hsuan Tsang, whose accounts are used to reconstruct its history. The 'Schools of Discussion' maintained a high standard of debate with well-known names of Mahāyāna Buddhism like Nāgārjuna and Śīlendrabodhi being present. For the upkeep of the monastery 200 villages had been set aside. The library comprised of three buildings, which was a great attraction. Tibetans started coming to Nālandā as early as Hsuan Tsang's time and one of the earliest to come was Thonmi Sambotha, sent by Songtsen Gampo.

Oḍantapurī : Was founded by Gopāla, the Pāla king developed into a great *mahāvihāra* by the Pāla times and was very near Nālandā. Oḍantapurī had a well-stocked library that was destroyed by the Turks in the eleventh century. Oḍantapurī served as the model for the famous Sam-ye monastery, the first monastery of Tibet.

Vikramaśilā: A famous centre of a Mahāyāna learning, Vikramaśilā had six colleges with many branches of study like logic, grammar, metaphysics and ritualistic practices. Like Nālandā, Vikramaśilā played a great part in the propa-gation of Buddhism to Tibet. Dīpaṅkara Śrījñāna reverently called Atiśa by the Tibetans was one of the leading lights of this university who spent thirteen years in Tibet and was a leading light in the Second Diffusion.

Somapura: Also a Pāla monastery and a famed *mahāvihāra* continued the great educational tradition of Nālandā with which there was considerable intercourse. According to Tibetan tradition where there are many references to Somapura in the *Blue Annals*, Atiśa and his Tibetan disciple Nag-tsho stayed here and translated a work by Bhavya before his departure to Tibet.

Jagaddala: The last great *mahāvihāra* founded by the Pāla kings was a great Tāntric centre and also a centre for translation which attracted many Tibetan scholars. Tibetan sources mention that many sections of the *Tangyur* and *Kangyur* were translated here. Bibhūti Candra, Dānaśīla and Mokṣakaragupta were the leading lights here. Jagaddala survived for some more years than Nālandā and Vikramaśilā according later visitors.

Ratnagiri: Situated on the eastern coast in Kaliṅga, Ratnagiri was a *mahāvihāra* patronised by the Bhaumakara rulers. Tārānatha the famous Tibetan historian mentions Ratnagiri as a centre where both Hīnayāna and Mahāyāna were undertaken. Recent excavations have revealed interesting findings.

Valabhi: Situated on the western coast of India, Valabhi was the most famous monastery of this area founded around AD 588. Located on a trade route, Valabhi was patronised by the Maitraka kings and wealthy merchants. Two disciples of Vasubandhu and Sthiramati were the leading lights of this university

Samye : The first Tibetan monastery was modelled on the famous Oḍantapurī *mahāvihāra*. The foundation of

Samye was laid during the time of Trisong Detsen who invited Śāntirakṣita to establish this monastery. Evil spirits and bad omens came up which stirred the hostility of the people forcing Śāntirakṣita to heat a hasty retreat.

On the advice of Śāntirakṣita, the king invited Padmasambhava who was well versed in Tantra. Padmasambhava subdued the malevolent spirits and Samye was finally built. Samye was built on the plan of a *maṇḍala* with the main structure having a mythical place of Buddha in the middle which was the very core of the universe. Four major and eight minor temples surrounded it. There were 1008 small *chortens*, 108 buildings and four main gates the last mentioned whose function was to stop evil spirits. Paṇḍita Nain Singh and L.A. Waddell had surveyed the ruins extensively.

Jokhang : Tibet's most sacred temple was built by Songtsen Gampo and predates the Samye monastery. It is called Tsuglag Khang and is a treasure trove of paintings and stuccos that have Nepālī and Gupta influences. The Jowo Lha Khang is the sanctum of the Jokhang enshrining a sacred image of Śākyamuni which pilgrims venerate by touching their forehead. Songtsen Gampo's chapel and the chapel of Phalden Lhamo the divine protectress of Tibet are other holy spots. There is also an inscribed pillar here.

Tholing: Situated in the extreme western part of Tibet, Tholing monastery was founded by Lotsba Rinchen Zangpo under the patronage of Yeshe Ö. The great Lotsba was the first abbot of this monastery. According to the biography of the lotsba, he met Atiśa here. The lotsba was old, around eighty-five years of age. Stylistically it follows the *maṇḍala* plan with orientation at four cardinal points and used of large quantities of timber. The main temple here is the Yeshe Ö temple, famous in Tibetan history as a great repository of Buddhist Tāntric works. In the *Dgra Scan Lha Khang* are sixteen stuccos of sixteen *arhats*. Tholing was the spring board from where the Buddhist revival started.

Tabo: Founded in AD 996, Tabo belongs to the age of Rinchen Zangpo. The full name of Tabo is Tabo Chos-Khor meaning the doctrinal enclave of Tabo situated in Spiti valley which formed part of the Guge Kingdom. Tabo is built on flat ground according to the *maṇḍala* plan typical of monasteries to the early period. All the temples here are located in linear symmetry. In the gTsug Lha Khang are found many paintings done in Ajantā style. The complete setting of the *du-Khang* describes the *Vajradhātu maṇḍala* (*r Dorje d Byings dkuil-h khar*). Tabo recently celebrated its centenary in 1996 AD.

Alchi: Situated in Ladakh, Alchi is said to have been founded by Rinchen Zangpo but some researchers credit Kaldan Shesrab with its founding. Alchi-chos-khor is an irregularly shaped enclosure consisting of small courtyards connected by narrow alleys in which are disposed the five main places of worship. Alchi is one of the richest *gompas* as far as paintings and stuccos are concerned, all done in Kāśmīrī style.

Śākya: As the name indicates, this monastery belongs to the Śākyapa sect and originally consisted of two large complexes, Śākya North and Śākya South. Kon Chogyal Pho founded Śākya North, which was originally a modest shrine, later to be enlarged by his son Kunga Nyingpo who was equally famous for his compilation of the religious doctrine Śākya Lamdre Chogyu. Śākya South was built by the Śākya Panchen on the orders of the famous Śākya patriarch, Phagpa shelves or cabinets called Kunga Rawa, contained the sacred Buddhist texts which amounted to around 20000 volumes. Particularly striking was a book called *Gyatong Pa,* a summary of the *Kangyur* and *Tangyur,* measuring 1.3 m by 1.1 m Śākya was also rich in paintings which numbered around 3000 *thanka*s of which 360 date from the Sung, Yuan and Ming dynasties. There are also 20000 rare sculptures including a statue of Mahākāla brought from Bodh-Gayā by *mahāsiddha* Birūpa.

Architecturally, the north monastery is a departure from monasteries of the eleventh century as it did not adhere to any plan but was built as a conglomeration of buildings, housing chapels, administrative buildings and defensive structures which make their appearance from the thirteenth when fortifications were started. Contrasting sharply to the north monastery is the south monastery that was virtually an impregnable fortress laid strictly according to a plan. At the centre is the *Lhakang Chenmo* around which are the *Lhakang Jangma, Labrang* and other buildings. The whole monastery has a massive wall, built of stone and mud birck, serving as model for central Tibetan monasteries. Śākya ranks next only to the great Gelugpa *gompa*s of Sera, Ganden, Drepung and Tashilhunpo in terms of size, collection of artefacts and books. Controlling vast tracts of land (around eleven enclaves), Śākya was never starved of funds.

Ramoche: Ramoche is historically associated with Wen Chang, who it is said to have divined at a particular place where the statue fell down and this was the place where Ramoche stands. Ramoche is interesting for the fact that as an early temple it had Chinese influences in architecture to a very great degree (sloping roofs), that were part of the original structure. Later rebuilt by Kunga Dondrup, was the assembly hall of the *Gyurto Dratshang,* Lhasa's upper Tāntric college. The *Dukhang* housed the Dalai Lama's throne.

Ganden: The foremost of the great Gelugpa monasteries was home to around two thousand monks. Ganden was founded in 1409 on the spot where Tsongkhapa first meditated. The main chapel of Ganden, the Tsokchen was built in 1421. In the *Ser Trikhang* of Ganden was the golden throne of Tsongkhapa. The sanctity of Ganden was due to Tsongkhapa being entombed here and in whose memory a daily morning service used to be held daily. In the *Serdhung lhakhang* (the gold tomb of Tsongkhapa) housed the most sacred relic of the monastery, a silver cherten later gilded by gold. Inside this chapel was a tent made of felt presented by the peak secretary of the Dalai Lama who was a Dzungar Mongol.

Drepung: The largest, and most populous of Tibet's monasteries was home to around 7,700 monks Drepung means rice heap and was derived from the Sanskrit word *Dhanyakaṭaka* which was the name of a *stūpa* in south India where the Buddha is said to have expounded the Kālacakra Tantra for the first time. Jamyang Choje founded Drepung in 1416. At its height during the time of the fifth Dalai Lama, there lived around 7700 monks. As a Gelugpa *gompa* Drepung was attacked by the king of Tsang in 1618 and the Dzungar Mongols. In the eighteenth century it became a power centre in Tibetan politics with the establishment of the Ganden Potrang. As a centre of learning, Drepung attracted talent from all over the Tibetan culture area who flocked here to study in the famous *Dratshangs,* which were seven in number. Out of this, three specialised in exoteric learning while the *Ngagpa Dratshang* specialised in esoteric learning. Medical learning was in the *Deyang Dratshang* dedicated to Sangye Menla, the Medicine Buddha.

Sera: Was founded in 1419 by Śākya Yeshe, a disciple of Tsongkhapa. As a big monastery, Sera had around 5000 monks, most of who were attracted to the various *Dratshangs* of which Sera Me and *Ngagpa Dratshang* are oldest structures. Sera Me taught novices and Sera Je the third *Dratshang,* the largest was reserved for wandering monks from Kham. Buddhist followed the clockwise sequence of circumambulation and in Sera they used to go in a regular sequence starting from Sera Me, *Ngagpa Dratshang,* Sera Je, *Handong Khangtsen, Tsockchen* and Tsongkhapa's hermitage. Of these the *Tsockchen* was the most important and impressive buildings comprising four storeys and had five *lhakhangs* where the murals of the guardian kings can be found. There was a debating courtyard at Sera Je Dratshang.

Tashilhunpo: Ranked next only to Sera, Ganden and Drepung was also a big Gelugpa *gompa* located in Tsang province was founded in 1447 by Gendun Drub, the first Dalai Lama, Tashilhunpo is the seat of the Tashi lama, popularly known as the Panchen Rinpoche (The Great Precious Teacher) who is regarded as the reincarnation of the Buddha Amitābha (Tib. *Wopame*). There were four *Dratshangs* in Tashilhunpo of which one college called the *Ngagpa Dratshang* was devoted to Tāntric studies. *Jamkhang Chenmo* (the palace of the Panchen Lamas, the *Khudung* and the *Kesang Lhakang* are the important buildings in the centre around which pilgrims circumambulate. The *Jamkhang Chemmo's* main attractions are the golden roof and a 26 metre high statue of Maitreya Buddha, *(Jampa)* made of around 300 kg of gold and 150 metric tons of copper liberally decorated with precious stones. There were around 4000 monks here.

Chakpori: Situated just on the outskirts of Lhasa, it attained fame as a famous monastery specialising in medicine. Located on a hill Chakpori had around 5000 rock carvings, the highest number in Tibet, portraying Śākyamuni, Chenresi, Guru Rinpoche, Tsongkhapa who were the culture heroes of Tibet. The medical college was established in 1695 under the sponsorship of Desi Sangye Gyatso, the regent of the fifth Dalai Lama. Chakpori soon emerged as a famous medical and astrological centre synthesising the various medical traditions of Tibet into a unified tradition. The *Menpa Dratshang* was the college here, which attracted talent from as far as Mongolia and Bhutan.

Shalu: A very famous monastery having a good collection of paintings belonging to the fourteenth century Newari style. It was founded in the eleventh century but rose to prominence only by the fourteenth century. Architecturally Shalu is a combination of Chinese and Tibetan styles. The Chinese styles were due to the patronage of the Yuan court. Shalu pioneered the later painiting style that was to exert a great influence all over Tibet for centuries to came. Arniko, the master painter from Kāṭhmāṇḍu was the pioneer of this art. Apart from painting, *lungom* (long distance running) and *tumo* (the generation of internal heat) were the esoteric disciplines practised in Shalu.

Gyantse: One of the biggest monastic towns, the famous relies of Gyantse were the massive temple of *Palkor Chode* and the *Kumbum chorten.* Gyantse was situated on a trade route and also a place of strategic importance, which is why it was well patronised and also open to influence from Nepal and China. The *Palkor Chode,* the great temple built by Rabtan Kunsang Phag between 1418 and 1925 was an imposing building painted in red. In the *Dukhang* was a painted image of Vairocana. The *chogyal lhakhang* contains a beautiful mural of the 11-faced Chenresi and another momental *gas-sku* portraying Śākyamuni among the *bodhisattavas*. The *chorten* at Gyantse was a massive structure that included functional interior chapels whose walls were adorned with murals. The devotee had to climb up from inside the hollow and as he went up he worshipped the delties who were painted on the eight-storey *chorten.*

Narthang : Was founded in 1153 by the Kadampa teacher Tumton Lodron Drakpa and belonged to the Narthangpa, a subject of the Kadampa. It emerged as a famous printing centre which supplied the whole Tibetan culture area with volumes of *Kangyur* and *Tangyur*. Narthang had many wood blocks with which the printing of the *Kangyur, Tangyur, Jātaka* tales of the Buddha and others were printed.

Mindroling : Like Narthang, Mindroling was also famous for crafts. Founded in 1676 by Terdag-Lirgpa Gyurmed Dorje, it was situated south of Lhasa. The fifth Dalai Lama granted all the authority and facilities for establishing this Nyingmapa monastery. It housed around 300 monks.

Thupten Dorjey Drag Evam Chogor: Also belonged to the Nyingmapa school. It was also known as Dorjey Drag and was one of the six famous Nyingmapa monasteries. Ngan Panchen Pema Wangyel founded this monastery in the sixteenth century. Apart form Sūtra and Tantra, medicine and astrology were taught here.

Tsurphu : It was the premier Kagyu monastery and their traditional seat of learning founded by the first Karmapa. Situated south of Lhasa at Tholung. Tsurphu emerged as a great centre for the study of the Sūtras and Tantras, particulary the teachings of Gampopa, which combined the two steams of *mahāmudrā* teachings with the Kadam teachings of the stages of the path.

Drukpa Sang Ngag Choling: The principal monastery of the Drukpa Kagyu tradition was founded by the third Drukchen Rinchoper, Jamyang Chakyi Drugpa. The Drukpa lineage is one of the eight minor Kagyu traditions.

Ngor: Belonged to the Śākyapa sect and was founded by Ngorchen Kunga Zangpo, who developed a new ritual style not fundamentally different from that of the Śākya sect but incorporated some special rituals. Ngor was noted for maintaining the 18 tunes which dated from the time of Rinchen Zangpo.

Labrang : One of the six biggest Gelugpa monasteries, Labrang was situated in Amdo. The first Jamyang Shayepa Nagavaga Tsondru founded it in 1710. He was a disciple of the fifth Dalai Lama it had six *Dratshangs* of which the largest was Meyying Thosmabing in which Sūtra and debate were studied. A 'Great Prayer Festival' with examination to award degrees was held every year. Labrang had nearly 4000 monks and 138 branch monasteries all over Tibet.

Tashi Menri: Was the main Bon monastery in Tibet, located at Tobgyal in Tsang. It was established in 1405 by Sheykb Gyaltsen and had four colleges Lingmey, Lingto, Lingkey and Lingzur. Menri had 250 branch monasteries all over Tibet except in the Ü and Tsang areas. Menri was home to around 500 monks who came from all over Tibet.

Appendix II

Tibetan Monasteries in India
(Established from 1959-91)

The monasteries of Nying-ma-pas

Mindroling: Ogyen Mindroling was the main *Nying-ma-pa* monastery in Tibet. At present, Mindroling has been re-established in Clement town, Uttar Pradesh, largely due to the efforts of Kochen Rinpoche. Minling Trichen Rinpochey is the present Throne Holder of Mindroling monastery. The Dalai Lama laid the foundation stone of a new college in 1988 and it was inaugurated in the spring of 1991.

Thepten Dorjey Drag Evam Chogar: It was the another famous monastery of Nyingma school, also known as Dorjey Drag. Dorjey Drag monastery has been re-established in Shimla, Himachal Pradesh, under the supervision of Taglung Tsetrul Rinpochey. It has close relation with the Namgyal, Nechung and Gadong, monasteries in Dharamśālā. The study and practice of Sūtra, Tantra and the traditional Buddhist fields of knowledge are pursued here. The emphasis is particularly on the practice of the various Tantras. The number of monks in this monastic centre is about 100. Many monks go for meditational retreats for long period.

Ugyen Ling Gompa: This monastery is established at Rabgye Ling Tibetan settlement, Hansur, Karnataka

State. Ugyen is considered as the birthplace of Guru Rinpoche. It has one branch at Orissa also. The number of monks is about 25 here.

Zongchen Rudham Samten Ling: It was a famous monastery in Tibet, established by Padma Rigdzis in 1685. It is re-established in Dhonden Ling Tibetan settlement, Kollegal, Karnataka State. Dzongchen Rinpoche is the chief abbot here who completed his education in Institute of Buddhist Dialectics, Dharamśālā. The number of monks in this monastery is about 50.

Tana Thekchok Norbuling: It is also established in Dhonden Ling Tibetan settlement, Kollegal, Karnataka, the number of monks is about 40.

Ogyen Samten Choling: It is a small monastery, established in the Dhonden Ling settlement. The number of monks is in this monastery is about 30.

Palyul Namdrol Ling: Palyul is the name of the place near Kham in Tibet, where this monastery was established in 1665. After coming into exile it has been re-established at Bylakuppe, Karnataka State, Penor-Rinpoche, the head of Nyingmapa, was the motivating power to establish this monastery. It has one branch in Darjeeling also. The number of monks in this monastery is about 100.

Zilnon Gompa: It is established at Dharamśālā Himachal Pradesh. It is a small monastery. The number of monks is not more than 10. In this monastery mostly monks are *ngagpa*s. They are busy in retreat and Tāntric practices.

Rigzin Namdorling: It is a small monastery established at Mcleod Ganj, Dharamśālā. The number of monks is about 20.

Pema Rigzin Ling: It is established at Dharamaśālā. The number of monks is not more than 15.

Chime Gatseling: It is small monastery established at Dharamśālā. The number of monks here is not more than 10.

Tsang Domas Namdo Ling: It is also a small monastery established at Dharamśāla, Himachal Pradesh. The number of monks is not more than 10.

Palyul Chokhor: It is a big monastery of the Nyingma's which has been re-established at Bir, Himachal Pradesh. The number of monks here is more than 200.

Choeling: It is established at Bir, Himachal Pradesh and famous as 'Bhutanese Institute'. The number of monks is about 60-70.

Evam choegar Gyurme Ling: It is established at Bir, District Kāṅgrā, Himachal Pradesh. The number of monks in this monastic centre is more than 100.

Thupten Dorje Drak: It has been established at Shimla, Himachal Pradesh. The number of monks is more than 50.

Himalayan Nyingma: Khenpo Thupten, at Manālī, Himachal Pradesh, established it. The number of monks is more than 50.

Kham Kathok Gompa: It was established by Kadampa Desheg in 1159 in Kham province. After 1954, it has been re-established at Solan, Himachal Pradesh. The number of monks is not more than 10.

Thupa Lhakhang: It is also a small monastery established at Poaṇṭā Sāhib, Himachal Pradesh. The number of monks is less than 10.

Dadul Rapten Ling: This has been re-established at Gajapati, Orissa. The number of monks is more than 40.

Thubten MindroLing: This has been also re-established at

Gajapati, Orissa. The number of monks is less than 50 in this monastery.

Ugyen Thekshok Ling: It is established in Phuntsok Ling Tibetan settlement Gajapati, Orissa. The number of monks here is about 30. The name of this monastery is after Ugyen Rinpoche, who was a very famous Nyingmapa scholar.

Tsang Domar Namdrol Ling: This monastery is named after the place name, Tsang Domar. It has been re-establsihed in Phuntsok Ling Tibetan settlement, Gajapati, Orissa. The number of monks is less than 15.

Gonjang Samten Choephuk: This monastery is named after the Gonjang Rinpoche. It has been re-established at Ranball, Darjeeling, West Bengal, Gonjang Samten is a small monastery. It is a branch monastery. It has an 'Art School for monks'. The main activity of this monastery is to provide the service of *Yung-me*. It also provides ritual practices for lay followers. The number of monks is around 20.

Phuntsok Pema Chokhor Ling: This monastery has been re-established at Darjeeling, West Bengal. It is a branch of Karnataka Nyingma Monastery. The chief abbot of this monastery is Khyebje Penor Rinpoche, who is also the head of Nyingma sect. This monastery provides the training of rituals to the Nyingma monks. The number of monks in this monastery is less than 40.

Ugyen Kunsang Chokhor Ling: This monastery is also esablished at Darjeeling, West Bengal. The number of monks in this monastery is about 50.

Phuntsok Nyayap Ling: This monastery has been re-established Darjeeling, West Bengal by Ven. Chatral Rinpoche. It is a small monastery. The number of monks in this monastery is not more than 20.

Zangdok Pelri: This monastery is established at Darjeeling. The number of monks in this monastery is less than 10.

Pema Choeling: This monastery is established at Mao in Choephel Ling Tibetan Settlement, Arunachal Pradesh. The number of monks in this monastery is not more than 40.

Ugyen Choeling: This monastery has been re-established in Dhargye Ling Tibetan settlement, Arunachal Pradesh. The number of monks in this monastery is less than 25.

Jang Chub Lhakhang: It is a small monastery established at Delhi. The number of monks in this monastery is only 15.

Guru Kubum Lhakhang: It is small monastery established at Gaṅgṭok, Sikkim. The number of monks in this monastery is only 5 or 6.

Nyedon Gatsel Ling: It is a big monastery of Nyingma sect established in Dehrādūn, Uttar Pradesh (now under Uttarāñcala) after 1959. The number of monks is more than 250 in this monastery.

Gepheling: This monastery is established in Kalimpong, West Bengal. The number of monks in the monastery is about 10. It is small monastery.

Dzongsar Institute: It is monastic college of Nyingma sect established at Bir, Himachal Pradesh after 1959. It has been established by Dzongsar Khenje Rinpoche, who is renowned as a non-sectarian Lama. The highest degree in this monastery is *Rabjampa*. The number of monks in this institute is more than 200 among them many are from Bhutan.

Tso Padma Nyingmapa Gonpa: This monastery has been established at Manālī, Himachal Pradesh. The number of monks in this monastery is about 10.

The monasteries of Kargyu-pas

Rumtek: The Tsurphu Monastery was the principal monastery of the Kargyu tradition in Tibet. The First Karmapa founded it. Tsurphu was the traditional seat of the line of Karmapas. It was situated to the north-west of Lhasa at Tolung. The tradition of Tsurphu has been re-established in Rumtek monastery. After coming into exile. Ranjung Riggey Dorje was appointed as the head of whole Kargyu tradition. He chose Rumtek Monastery to be his seat in exile. The tradition of Tsurphu was resumed and the monastery was rebuilt in 1969. It has become the biggest centre of Kargyu tradition. The Karma-Kargyu monasteries in India, Nepal, and Bhutan send two monks each to train in the Sūtra teachings through the medium of debate at this institute. The Karma Sri Nalanda Institute has one branch in Delhi also.

Drikungthil Ogmin Jangchubling: Drikung Kyobpa Jigten Gonpa Rinchenpel founded this monastery. It was located 150 km to the east of Lhasa. It has been re-established in India. Its traditions have been revived since 1989 at Dehrādūn, Uttar Pradesh (now under Uttarāñcala) the Jangchubling Drinkung Kargyu Institute. The number of monks in this institute is about 200.

Drukpa Sang Ngag Choling: It was the principal monastery of the Drukpa Kagyu Tradition. The third Drukchen Rinpoches, Jamyang Chokyi Drugpa, founded it. The Drukpa lineage is one of the eight minor Kargyu traditions deriving from disciples of Ragmo Trupa. After coming into exile, the Sang Ngag Choling monastery has been re-established in Darjeeling, West Bengal. It is re-established by the twelfth Drukchen Rinpoche. The monks at Snag Ngag Choling are trained in the teachings of Drukpo Kagyu lineage. The number of monks in this monastic centre is more than 200.

Thupten Shedup Jangchubling: This monastery has been re-established in Bylakuppe, Karnataka. The number of monks in this monastery is about 120. The chief abbot in this monastery is Ge Ayang Rinpoche.

Dri-kargyu: It is a very small monastery which is located at Majnu Kā Ṭīlā, Delhi. The number of monks in this monastery is not more than 10.

Thupten Samphel Ling: It is a small monastery established at Muṇḍgod, Karnataka. The number of monks in this monastery is not more than 50.

Rigon Samdup Chasthar: It is a small monastery established at Kollegal, Karnataka State. The number of monks is about 75.

Sherab Ling: This monastery is established at Upper Bhattu, Kāṅgrā district, Himachal Pradesh in 1980. This monastery is related to Situ Rinpoche, one of the four regents heading the Karma-kagyu tradition. The number of monks in this monastic centre is more than 100.

Karma Shedrup Dhargye Ling: Beru Khyentse Rinpoche established this monastery in 1989 at Bodh-Gayā, Bihar. The number of monks is not more than 50.

Tashi Choeling: It is very small monastery established in Dhramśālā, Himachal Pradesh. The number of monks in this monastery is about 20. The monasteries of Dukpa Kagyu tradition and it are established by Thah-Lama in 1986.

Chime Drupe Gastel: This monastery is established in Kullū, Himachal Pradesh. The number of monks in this monastery is about 40.

Zilnon Dhargye Lhakhang: It is a small monastic centre established at Mcleod Ganj, Dharamśālā. The number of monks is not more than 20. They are mostly engaged in Tāntric retreat. This monastery is established by Zilnon Dhargye. He is the main Lama of this monastic centre. This monastery is related with Karma-kargyu tradition.

U-rse Tithoe: This monastery is established at Rewalsar, Himachal Pradesh. The number of monks in this monastery is about 50.

Drukpa-Kargyu Ling: This is small monastery established in Rewalsar, Himachal Pradesh. The number of monks in this monastery is about 25.

Zigar Drukpa Institute: This monastery is established at Rewalsar, Himachal Pradesh. In this institute, the number of monks is about 75.

Phuntsok Chokhorling: This was very famous monastic centre of Kargyu tradition in eastern Tibet. It has been re-established by Khamtu-Rinpoche at Bir. The abbot of this monastery is Khenpo Dorzong. It is a monastery of Dukpa Kargyu tradition. In this monastery one nunnery project is also going on, where more than 30 nuns are getting education.

Thupten Sang-ngas Choling: It was a very important monastery, which was established in Tibet by Padma Karpa. In India, this monastic centre is re-established at Darjeeling, West Bengal. The number of monks in this monastic centre is more than 200. Thug-Se Rinpoche established it in 1960. This monastery is of Dukpa Kargyu tradition.

Samdup Dhargye ling: This is also a very important monastic centre of Kargyu tradition. This is re-established at Darjeeling, West Bengal. The number of monks in this institution is more than 200.

Bokor Nyedon Choekher: This monastery has been

established at Darjeeling. The number of monks in this monastery is more than 80.

Drupgyu Choeling: This monastery is established at Bhandara resettlement colony, Maharashtra. The number of monks in this monastery is not more than 15. It is a small monastery.

Karma-Dhargye Chokhorling: This monastery is established at Bodh-Gayā, Bihar. It is small monastic centre where the number of monks is about 60.

Dharma Chakra Centre: Dharma Chakra Centre is established at Gaṅgṭok, Sikkim. The number of monks in this monastery is around 100.

Tsechok Ling: This is a small monastery established aslo at Gaṅgṭok, Sikkim The number of monks in this monastery is not more than 30.

Dechen Chokhor Ling: It is a small monastery established at Clement-Town Dehrādūn, Uttar Pradesh (now under Uttarāñcala). It is located near the main Nyingma Monastery. The number of monks in this monastery is not more than 50. Though it is a Kargyu monastic centre but one high lama Druk Chogan Rinpoche, from this monastery has been educated in the Institute of Buddhist Dialectics that is considered a Gelugpa institute.

Drikung Institute: It is small monastery re-established at Dehrādūn, Uttar Pradesh (now under Uttarāñcala). This monastery is related with Phe-Yang Gonpa located at Ladakh. It is a small monastic centre where the number of monks is not more than 20.

The monasteries of Śākya-pas

Śākya: In 1073, Kon Chogyal Pho (1034-1102) of the Khon family established the Palden Śākya Monastery in the Tsang province of Central Tibet. In India, the traditions of Śākya monastery, have been continued at the Śākya centre in Uttar Pradesh. It was founded by the present forty-first abbot of Śākya monastery and 'Holder of the Śākya Throne', Śākya Trizin.

In order to maintain the living tradition of the Śākya teachings, to promote higher education and extensive philosophical training, Śākya centre has established its educational programme. Outstanding monks receive high level training in Tantra, Sūtra and common subjects. After receiving education, they return to their branch monasteries to serve as instructors. They are also assigned to other positions of responsibility within the Śākya Order. Presently, the number of monks in this college is about 250.

Phenpo Nalendra Monastery: Nālandā monastery was established in the Phenpo district of Central Tibet in 1425 by the great Śākya master, Rongton Sheja Kunrig (1367-1459) and his disciple Kunkhyen Tashi Namgyel. Originally Nālandā had four colleges, Thongmon, Dukhor, Tshegye and Tshezhi. The tradition of Nālandā has been re-established in India after coming into exile.

Ngor: After coming into exile the tradition of Ngor monastery has been continued in Palsa Ngor Tsar Sum monastery. It has been re-established in Munṇḍgod, Karnataka. Since its establishment, it has been working as monastic college. Khempo Jamyang Tenzin is the incharge of academic programme. The number of monks is more than 100 in this monastic centre.

Śākya College: Śākya College was established to continue the study of Śākyapa monks. It is a modern educational institute. The number of monks is more than 100. It is established at Dehrādūn, Uttar Pradesh (now under Uttarāñcala). Khenpo Migmar Tsering was appointed as the head of the Śākya College in 1989.

Phureng Shedphel Ling: Phureng is the name of a place near Guge in Tibet. This monastery is established in Muṇḍgod. The number of monks is only 20 to 30. This monastery is associated with Śākya college. It is a small monastery.

Samdup Dechen Choekhor: It is established at Bir, Himachal Pradesh. The number of monks is about 80.

Drongsar Institute: This institute has been re-established at Bir, Himachal Pradesh. Dvongsar Khenje Rinpoche, who is renowned as a non-sectarian Lama, founded it. It is working as a monastic college and more than 200 monks are getting education in this institute.

Tsechen Ling: It is a small monasery established at Kumrao, Himachal Pradesh. The number of monks is more than 50.

Thupten Namgyal Ling: It is small monastery established at Puruwala, Uttar Pradesh. The number of monks is about 250.

Ngor Dal Evam Choden: It has been established at Prem Nagar, Dehrādūn, Uttar Pradesh (now under Uttarāñcala). The number of monks is about 250.

Tirkey Gompa Jang: It is small monastery established at Gaṅgṭok, Sikkim. The number of monks is about 30.

Sangor Chotsok: This monastery is also established at Gaṅgṭok, Sikkim. It is a small monastery. The number of monks is about 50.

Goom Guru Gon: This monastery at re-established in Darjeeling, West Bengal. It is also a small monastery. The number of monks is about 65.

Bir Śākya Lama's School: This is a small school established in the District Kāṅgrā, Himachal Pradesh. The number of student monks here is about 50.

Monasteries of Gelugpa Sect

Ganden: In exile, Ganden monastery has been re-established in Muṇḍgod, Karnataka State. It is comprised of two college Jangtsey and Shartsey, meaning 'North peak and East peak' respectively. Every college has different houses called Khamtsen and every Khamtsen has its own small assembly hall. Jangtsey college has twelve Khamtsens and Shartsey College has eleven divisions. There is one common hall called *Lachi* for worship. In Ganden monastery Sūtra and Tantra are taught to the monks of both colleges in a combined course. On the whole, Jangtsey is primarily responsible for Guhyasamāja rituals, while Shartsey maintains primarily the Vajrabhairava rituals. Other divisions within the two colleges are responsible for the rituals of other specific Tāntric deities from the four class of Tantra. For example, one Khangtsen in Shartsey maintains the Kālacakra rituals.

The position of Ganden Tripa is alternated between the Jangtsey Choje and the Shartsey Choje (Dharma Master of Jangtsey or Shartsey). The Jangtsey Choje is the senior retired abbot of Gyuto Tantric College. While the Shartsey, Choje, is the most senior retired abbot of Gyuto Tantric College. The number of monks in Ganden monastic University is about 3000.

Sera: The monastery of Sera was the second largest in Tibet. The tradition of Sera has been re-established in Bylakuppe, Karnataka. Colleges, Sera Je and Sera Me have been re-established. The number of monks in this monastic university is more than 3000. Hundreds of monks, from other countries are also studying in this monastery.

Dre-pung: It was the largest monastery in the world and situated about three and one-half miles from the western gate of Lhasa. The tradition of Drepung monastery has been re-established in exile at Muṇḍgod Karnataka. The number of monks getting monastic training, is more than 3000. It has been largest monastic centre of Tibetans in exile.

Tashi-Lhunpo: Gendun Durub, the first Dalai Lama, built the monastery of Tashi-Lhunpo in 1447. In exile the tradition of Tashi-Lhunpo has been re-established. The monastery has been re-established in Karnataka. The highest degree in this monastery is *Kachen-La*. There is about 200 monks, getting spiritual training in this monastery.

Gyumey: Gyumey, the lower Tāntric monastery, was founded by Sherab Sengey, a disciple of Je-Tson Khapa in AD 1440, in the southern Part ot Lhasa. The tradition of Tantra study of Gyumey has been re-established in Hunsur. More than 200 monks are getting spiritual training here. The main topics of study at Gyumey are the Tāntric system of Akṣobhaya from the Guhyasamāja. The Luipa tradition of *cakrasaṁvara* and the thirteenth diety Vanjrabhairva. The textbooks followed in this monastery are by Gyu Sherab Senge. The monks also study Tāntric rituals, art and music.

The Dalai Lama's Namgyal monastery follows the lineages and style of Gelug tradition. The Tāntric colleges at Sera and Drepung monasteries, known as Sera and Drepung Ngagpas, have a close relationship with Gyumey monastery.

Gyutod: Gyachen Kunga Dondrub established Gyutod, the upper Tāntric monastery. After coming into exile, the tradition of Gyutod has been established at Bomdila, Arunachal Pardesh. Monks from other Gelugpa monasteries come to study and practice of Tantra. The number of monks is more than 500.

Labrang Tashi Khyil Gomang: It was counted among six major monasteries of the Gelug Traidition. The monastery came to be known as 'Labrang Tashikhyil' in reference to Jamyang Shyapas residence. 'Labrang' means the residence of a great Lama. The tradition of 'Labrang' has been re-established in India after coming into exile. It has been established in Dehrādūn, Uttar Pradesh (now under Uttarāñcala). The number of monks is more than 200.

Namgyal: The third Dalai Lama founded The Namgyal Monastery in the sixteenth century AD. It was situated at Lhasa in Tibet. It was known as the monastery of the Dalai Lama, from this monastery monks were taken to dance and celebrate other functions for the Dalai Lama. It was also destroyed by Chinese invasion in 1959. It has been re-established at Dharamśālā, Himachal Pradesh. Presently, the number of monks is more than 150.

Ne-Chung Drayanling: It was the seat of the Nechung Oracle, one of the most important state oracles of Tibet, and closely associated with the Dalai Lama. It was located at Lhasa. Nechung is supposed to fall into a trance and pronounce his prophecy. It is consulted by Tibetan administration to take any important decision regarding Tibetan people in India.

Sangye Choeling: This monastery is established in Shimla, Himachal Pradesh. The number of monks is only 12.

Phuntsok Ling Nyentsampa: It is established in Dalhousie, Himachal Pradesh. It is a small monastery. The number of monks is about 20 only.

Dechen Chokhor Ling: It is established in Gajapati, Orissa. It is also a small monastery. The number of monks is only 12 here.

Zeikar Chode: This monastery is also established in Darjeeling, West Bangel. The number of monks in this monastery is about 20. It is a small monastery.

Sandryo Ogarygo Ling: This is a small monastery established at Darjeeling, West Bengal. The number of monks is about 10-15.

Samten Choeling: Samten Choeling was very important monastery in Tibet. It has been re-established at Darjeeling, West Bengal by Thumo-Geshe Rinpoche. The chief abbot of this monastery is Thumo-Geshe Rinpoche.

Gum Samten Choeling: This monastery is established in Darjeeling, West Bengal, Gumjang Rinpoche established this monastery. The head Lama has been staying in USA. It is a small monastery. The number of monks in this monastery is not more than 30.

Ganden Tashi Choeling: This monastery was in Amdo before 1959. It was a famous monastery. After coming into exile, it has been re-established in Darjeeling, West Bengal. It is a small monastery. The number of monks here is less than 15.

Sukhe Tashi Choeling: This is a small monastery established in Darjeeling, West Bengal. The number of monks is only 15-20.

Kurseong Tashi Choeling: It is also in Darjeeling. The number of monks is only 8-10 here. It is a small monastery.

Sed-Gyu Dastsang: It is established at Kalimpong, Darjeeling, West Bengal. The number of monks here is about 25-30.

Gaden Tharpa Choling: It is a small monastery, established at Kalimpong, West Bengal. The number of monks is 30-35. There is one temple of Dorje Shuden in this monastery. The chief abbot of this monastery has been staying in USA.

Thekchen Ling: It is a small monastery established in Norgyeling Tibetan Settlement Bhandhara,

Maharashtra. The number of monks is only 12-15.

Dro-Ngakpa Dratsang: It is a small monastery, established at Majnu Kā Ṭīlā, Delhi. The number of monks is only 10.

Gaden Phegye Ling: This monastery is established in Bodh-Gayā, Bihar. The number of monks is 55-60.

Thupten Shedup Dhargye Ling: It is a small monastery established in Bodh-Gayā, Bihar. The number of monks is only 6-10.

Gaden Chokhorling: It is a small monastery established in Gaṅgṭok, Sikkim. The number of monks is only 8-10.

Gomang Omang Tashi Khil: It is re-established in Thondup ling Tibetan settlement. Clement Town, Dehrādūn, Uttar Pradesh (now under Uttarāñcala). Gomang is related with Drepung monastery. The number of monks is about 25-30 in this monastery and most of them belong to Amdo.

Shedup Choeling: It is a small monastery established in Clement town. The number of monks is only 20-5.

Phuntsok Chopheling: It is also a small monastery, established in Dehrādūn. The number of monks is only 2-5.

Bon monasteries

Tashi Menri: Menri monastery was the main Bon Monastery in Tibet. It was located at Tobgyal in Tsang. It was established in 1405 by Sherub Gyaltsen. It has four colleges, Lingmey, Lingto, Lingkey and Lingzur. In 1969, the debate college of Menri, Pal Shenten Menri Ling has been re-established at Solan, Himachal Pradesh, Tenzin Nambak was driving force behind the re-establishment of Menri monastery in India. The main temple, the foundation of which was laid in 1969 was completed in 1978 and named Pelshenton

Menri Ling. The main temple is re-established for the pursuit of a strict monastic life, education of monks, performance of religious ceremonies, to maintain the major Tāntric rituals of Bon and to preserve the cultural heritage of Tibet. There are three groups in the main monastery at Solan. The first group consists of Lamas and monks who came from Tibet. They perform ceremonies in the houses of laymen and participate in all the rituals, which take place in the monastery. The second group consists of young men who took their religious vows in this monastery. They are being educated in the Bonpo doctrines and trained to live according to Bonpo monastic rules.

The third group consists of boys between seven and fourteen years old. They receive primary education in the school near the monastery. They also receive instructions in religion, Tibetan calligraphy, painting and music and take part in the all ceremonies in the monastery.

Bibliography

Primary Sources

The Blue Annals, part one, Roerich, George N., Calcutta, Royal Asiatic Society of Bengal, 1949.

Vinaya Texts — The *Mahavagga*, V, X.

The *Cullavagga* I-III

The *Cullavagga*, IV-XII

Tr. from Pāli By T.W. Rhys, Davids and Hermann Oldenberg, part II.

Ex Max Muller, *Sacred Books of the East*, vol. XVII, New Delhi, Motilal Banarsidass, 1965.

Books

An-Che, Li, *History of Tibetan Religion: A Study in the Field*, Beijing, New World Press, 1994.

An-Che, Li, ed. Nakane, Chie, *Labrang A Study in the Field*, Tokyo, University of Tokyo, 1982.

Ancient Tibet (Tibetan history Series, V) Research Materials from the Yeshe De Project, California, Dharma Publishing Co., 1986.

Bell, Charles, *The People of Tibet*, New Delhi, Asian Educational Services, 1991.

Bell, Charles, *The Religion of Tibet*, New Delhi, Asian Educational Services, 1992.

Bell, Charles, *Tibet: Past and Present*, New Delhi, Asian Educational Services, 1992.

Bhattacharya, Dilip, *Bhutan*, New Delhi, Oxford and IBH, 1975.

Birnbaum, Raoul, *The Healing Buddha*, London, Rider and Rider Company, 1979.

Burman, Bina Roy, *Religion and Politics in Tibet*, New Delhi, Vikas, 1979.

Casinelli, C.W. and Ekvall, Robert B., *A Tibetan Principality, The Political System of Saskya*, Ithaca, Cornell University Press, 1969.

Chan, Victor, *Tibet Handbook*, California, Moon Publications, 1994.

Chapman, F. Spencer, *Lhasa: The Holy City*, London, Readers Unon, 1940.

Coleman Graham, ed., *A Handbook of Tibetan Culture*, New Delhi, Rupa and Co, 1995, rpt.

Daniel, Perdue, *Introductory Debate in Tibetan Buddhism*, Dharmasala, LTWA 1976.

Dorjee, Pema, *Stupa and its Technology: A Tibeto-Buddhist Perspective*, New Delhi, Indira Gandhi National Centre for Arts and Molital Banarsidass, 1996.

Dutt, Sukumar, *Buddhist Monks and Monasteries of India*, London, Allen and Unwin, 1962.

Fisher, Robert, E, *Buddhist Art and Architecture*, London, Thomes and Hudson, 1993.

Fundamentals of Tibetan Medicine According the RGYUD-BZHI, Dharmasala Men-Tse-Khang, Tibetan Medical and Astrological Institute of H.H. the Dalai Lama, 1995, 2nd rev. edn.

Fundamentals of Tibetan Medicine, Dharmasala, Men-Tse-Khang, 1995.

Gyatsho, Thubten Legshay, *Gateway to the Temple*, H.K. Kuloy, tr. David Paul Jackson, Kathmandu, Ratna Pustak Bhandar, 1979.

Handa, O.C., *Buddhist Monasteries in Himachal Pradesh*, New Delhi, Indus Publishing Co. 1987.

Hugh Richardson, ed. Michael Aris, *Ceremonies of the Lhasa Year*, London, Serindia Publications, 1993.

Holdich, Thomas, *Tibet, The Mysterious*, London, Alston Rivers, 1908.

Jiawei, Wang and Gyaincain, Nyima, *The Historical Status of China's Tibet*, Beijing, China Intercontinental Press, 1997.

Khosla, Romi, *Buddhist Monasteries in the Western Himalayas*, Kathmandu, Ratna Pustak Bhandar, 1979.

Khangkar, Lady Dr. Lobsang Dolma, ed. K. Dhondup, *Lectures on Tibetan Medicine*, Dharamasala, LTWA, 1986.

Lauf, Detlef Ingo, *Tibetan Sacred Art: The Heritage of Tantra,* Berkeley, Shambala 1976.

MacDonald (David), *Cultural Heritage of Tibet*, New Delhi, Light and Life Publishers, 1978.

Michael, Franz, *Rule by Incarnation: Tibetan Buddhism and its Role in Society And State*, Boulder, Westview Press, 1982.

Miller, Robert James, *Monasteries and Culture Change in Inner Mongolia*, Wiesbaden, Otto Harrassowitz, 1991.

Norbu, Dawa, *Tibet: The Road Ahead*, New Delhi, Harper Collins Publishers, India, 1997.

Norbu, Namkhai, *The Necklace of gzi — A Cultural History of Tibet*, Dharamasala, Narthang Publications, 1989.

Neel-Alexandra David, *Magic and Mystery in Tibet*, New Delhi, Harper Collins Publishers India Pvt Ltd., 1993.

Pal, Pratapaditya, *Tibetan Paintings — A Study of Tibetan Thankas Eleventh to Nineteenth Centuries*, New Delhi, Times Books International, 1988.

Paltu, Lama/Lodoe, Jampal, *Record of Nyingma Monasteries in Tibet*, Dalhousie, n.d.

Rahul, Ram, *Government and Politics of Tibet*, Delhi, Vikas, 1969.

Rahul, Ram, *Dalai Lama — The Institution*, Delhi, Vikas, 1995.

Richardson, H.E., *Tibet and its History*, London, Oxford University Press, 1962.

Rizvi, Janet, *Ladakh Crossroads of High Asia*, New Delhi, Oxford University Press, 1996.

Samuel, Geoffrey, *Civilized Shamans Buddhism in Tibetan Socieries*, London, Smithsonian Institution Press, 1993.

Schlagintweit, Emil, *Buddhism in Tibet*, London, Susil Gupta, 1968, rpt.

Shakabpa, Tsepon W.D., *Tibet — A Political History*, New York, Potala Publications, 1988.

Sharma, R.S., *Material Culture and Social Formations in Ancient India*, Madras, Macmillan, 1992.

Shen, Tsung, Lien and Liu, Shen-Chien, *Tibet and the Tibetans*, Stanford, Stanford University Press, 1953.

Sinha, Nirmal C., *Tales The Thankas Tell — An Introduction to Tibetan Scroll Portraits*, Gangtok, Sikkim Research Institute of Tibetology, 1989.

Snellgrove, David L. and Skorupski, Tadeusz, *The Cultural Heritage of Ladakh*, New Delhi, Vikas Publishing House, 1977.

Snellgrove, David and Richardson, Hugh, *Cultural History of Tibet*, London, George Weidenfeld and Nicholson, 1968.

Stein, R.A., tr. J.E. Stapleton Driver, *Tibetan Civilisation*, London, Faber and Faber Ltd., 1972.

Tucci, Giuseppe, *Tibet — Land of Snows*, New Delhi, Oxford and IBH Co., 1967.

Waddell, L.A., *The Buddhism of Tibet or Lamaism*, New Delhi, Asian Educational Services, 1991.

Zysk, Kenneth G., *Asceticism and Healing in Ancient India*, Delhi, Oxford University Press, 1991.

Ph.D. Thesis

Aggarwal, Ajay Kumar, A *Study of the Establishment of Tibetan Monasteries in India From 1959-1991*, Ph.D. Thesis, University of Delhi, New Delhi, 1997.

Ghosh, Krishna, *Few Tibetan Deities,* Unpublished Ph.D. Thesis, University of Delhi, New Delhi, 1996.

Melpittiye, Venerable Wimalakitti, *A Comparative Analysis of Symbolism in Theravada and Mahayana Iconography*, Unpublished Ph.D. Thesis, University of Delhi, New Delhi, 1996.

Tsarong Paljor, *Economy and ideology on a Tibetan Monastic estate in Ladakh : Process of Production, reproduction and transformation*, Ph.D. Thesis University of Wisconsin Madison, Ann Arbor, Michigan UMI Dissertation Services, 1993.

Articles

'Anonymous', *Tibetan Review*, New Delhi, vol. II, September 1976, p. 23.

'Butter Sculpture', *Choyang*, no. 2, 1987.

'Divination in Tibet' *Choyang*, no. 6, 1994.

Barmark, Jan, 'Tibetan Buddhist Medicine from the perspective of Anthropology of knowledge', *Tibetan Medicine*, series no. 13, 1991.

Brue, Erberto, F. Lo, 'The Sacred Enclave of Gyantse' in Pal, Pratapaditya, ed., Marg Publication, *A Pot Pourri of Indian Art,* Bombay, *Marg*, vol. XLVII, no. 4, 1998.

Chapela, Leonard R., 'Economic Institutions of Buddhist Tibet', *The Tibet Journal*, vol. XVII, no.3, Autumn 1992.

Dagthon, Prof Jampa G., 'An introduction to Tibetan Astro Science', Kalsang, Jampa, tr., *Tibetan Astronomy and Astrology — a brief introduction*, Dharmasala, Astro Department, Tibetan Medical and Astro Institute, 1995.

Das, S.C., 'The Monasteries of Tibet reprinted from *JASB*, 1905 in Chattopadhya, Alaka, ed., *Tibetan Studies*, Delhi, Motilal Banarsidass, 1984.

Dash, Vaidya Bhagwan, 'Ayurveda in Tibet', *The Tibet Journal*, Dharmasala, LTWA, vol. I, 1975-6.

Dash, Vaidya Bhagwan, 'Ayurveda in Tibet', *The Tibet Journal*, Dharmasala, vol. 1, no. 1, July/September 1975.

Dorji, Dr.Pema, 'Introductory Notes on Tibetan Medicine', ed. Jeremy Russel, *Tibetan Medicine*, series no. 12, 1984.

Gelek, Surkhang Wangchen, 'Government Monastic and Private Taxation in Tibet', *Tibet Journal*, vol. X, no.1, Spring 1986.

Goldstein, Melvyn C. and Tsarong, Paljor, 'Tibetan Buddhist Monasticism: Social, Psychological and Cultural implications', *The Tibet Journal*, vol. X, no. 1, Spring 1985.

Goldstein, Melvyn. C., 'Reexamining Choice, Dependency and Command in the Tibetan Social System: Tax Appendages and other Landless Serfs', *The Tibet Journal*, vol XI, no. 4, Winter 1986.

Gombo, Ugen, 'The Traditional Tibetan Economy. An overview Analysis from a Socio-Anthropological perspective', *Tibetan Review*, vol., 13, February-March 1978.

Hess, Michael, 'Early Tibetan Sculpture' in Pal, Pratapaditya, ed., Marg Publication, *A Pot Pourri of Indian Art*, Bombay, *Marg*, vol. XLVII, no. 4, 1998.

Jain, Sirish, 'Traditional Healing and Modern Medical Facilities among an Indo Tibetan Community, A brief ethno medical survey of the Bodhs of Spiti, *S Man rtsis*, Dharmasala, LTWA, vol. 11, no. 11, 1996.

Janes Craig, R., 'The Transformations of Tibetan Medicine' *Medical Anthropology Quarterly*, New York, vol. 9, no. 1, March 1995.

Joshi, C.V., 'Life and Teachings' in Bapat, P.V., ed., *2500 years of Buddhism*, New Delhi, Publications Division, 1997.

Kaldhen, Jampel, 'Interest Rates in Tibet', *The Tibet Journal*, vol. 1, no. 1, July/September 1975.

Kalsang, Jhampa, 'A brief introduciton to rSipa-Ho' in *Tibetan Astronomy and Astrology — A brief introduction*, Dharmasala, Astro Department, Tibetan Medical and Astro Institute, 1995.

Kalsang, Jhampa, Kachupa, Tsipa, 'Traditional Community Role of the Astro Practitioner' in *Tibetan Astronomy and Astrology — A brief introduction*, Dharmasala, Astro Department, Tibetan Medical and Astro Institute, 1995.

Kapsner, Mathew, 'Thanka Painting', *Choyang,* Dharmasla, an occasional publication of the Department of Culture of H.H. the Dalai Lama, no. 3, 1993.

Karmay, Prof Samten G., 'Vairocana and the rGyud-bZhi', *Tibetan Medicine*, series no. 12, 1989.

Lodro, Kalden T. and Russell, Jermey, 'Namgyal Monastery', *Choyang*, no. 3, 1993.

Rabgay, Lobsang, 'The origin and growth of Medicine in Tibet', *Tibetan Medicine*, Dharamasala, LTWA, series no. 3, 1994.

Ray, Reginald A., 'Some Aspects of the Tulku Tradition in Tibet', *The Tibet Journal*, vol. XI, no. 4, Winter 1986.

Reynolds, Valrae, 'Fabric images and their special role in Tibet' in Pal, Pratapaditya, ed., Marg Publication, *A Pot Pourri of Indian Art*, Bombay, *Marg*, vol. XLVII, no. 4, 1998.

Richardson, Hugh E., 'Political Role of the Four Sects in Tibetan History', *Tibetan Review*, vol. 17, September 1976.

Semple, William, 'Symbolism and Ritual in Tibetan Architecture', *Choyang*, no. 5

Shakya, Tsering, Rabgyas, Tashi and Crook, John, 'Monastic Economics in Zangskar, 1980' in Crook John H., and Osmaston Henry A., ed., *Himalayan Buddhist Villages*, New Delhi, Motilal Banarsidass, 1994.

Singer, Jane Casey, 'Early Thankas Eleventh-Thirteenth Centuries' in Pal, Pratapaditya, ed., Marg Publication, *A Pot Pourri of Indian Art*, Bombay, *Marg*, vol. XLVII, no. 4, 1998.

Sithar, Kunchok, 'Tibetan Monastic life in the past and present', *Tibetan Review*, vol. 24, March 1989.

Smith, Warren W., 'The Ideological Basis of China's Tibet Policy', *Tibetan Review*, vol. 23, November 1989.

'The Geshe Degree' *Choyang,* no. 2, 1987.

'The Geshe Degree', *Choyang,* no. 4

'The Throwing of Ritual Cakes' *Choyang*, no. 2, 1987.

'The Vajra Bell and Beads', *Choyang*, no. 2, 1987.

Tulku, Sherpa, Tulku, Khamlung, Berzing Alexander and Landaw, Jonathan 'The structure of the Ge-lug Monastic order', *The Tibet Journal*, vol. II, no. 3, Autumn, 1977.

Wangdi, Dr. Sonam and Dr. Philip, 'Astrological Tradition of Tibet, Part-I History', *Tibetan Review*, New Delhi, vol. 14, October 1979.

Wangdi, Dr. Sonam and Dr. Philip, 'Astrological Tradition of Tibet, Part-II Almanac and Calendar', *Tibetan Review*, vol. 14, December 1979.

Index